TREXLER LIBRARY

JUN 0 1 2001

DeSales University
Center Valley, PA 18034

THE AUTOBIOGRAPHY OF
WILLIE O'REE
HOCKEY'S BLACK PIONEER

Willie O'Ree
with Michael McKinley

SOMERVILLE HOUSE, USA
NEW YORK

Copyright © 2000 Willie O'Ree

ISBN:1-58184-071-3   A B C D E F G H I J

Printed in Canada

Writers: Willie O'Ree and Michael McKinley
Designer: fiwired.com

Somerville House, USA, is distributed by
Penguin Putnam Books for Young Readers
345 Hudson Street, New York, NY 10014

Published in Canada by
Somerville House Publishing
a division of Somerville House Books Limited
3080 Yonge Street, Suite 5000
Toronto ON M4N 3N1

e-mail: sombooks@goodmedia.com
Web site: www.sombooks.com

Photo Credits
Photo insert section, in order of appearance:
Willie O'Ree's Personal Collection; Hockey Hall of Fame; Imperial Oil-Turofsky/ Hockey Hall of Fame; Bruce Bennett Studios; Willie O'Ree's Personal Collection; Hockey Hall of Fame; Willie O'Ree's Personal Collection; Willie O'Ree's Personal Collection; Willie O'Ree's Personal Collection; Los Angeles Times (Lori Shepler)
Front cover: Willie O'Ree's Personal Collection
Back cover: Willie O'Ree's Personal Collection

Every effort has been made to trace the copyright holders, and we apologize in advance for any unintentional omissions. We would be pleased to insert the appropriate acknowledgment in any subsequent edition of this publication.

All NHL logos and marks, and team logos and marks depicted herein are the property of the NHL and the respective teams and may not be reproduced without the prior written consent of NHL Enterprises L. P. © 2000 NHL. All rights reserved.

CONTENTS

CHAPTER ONE:	The First Step Forward	7
CHAPTER TWO:	Home	12
CHAPTER THREE:	School Days	18
CHAPTER FOUR:	Gone Fishing	24
CHAPTER FIVE:	My Star Starts to Rise	27
Chapter SIX:	Game Over?	32
CHAPTER SEVEN:	Play Ball?	38
CHAPTER EIGHT:	The Dream Comes True	44
CHAPTER NINE:	Battling Racism	50
CHAPTER TEN:	The Jackie Robinson of Hockey	53
CHAPTER ELEVEN:	Waiting	60
CHAPTER TWELVE:	The Black Bear	66
CHAPTER THIRTEEN:	The Black Bear Fights Back	71
CHAPTER FOURTEEN:	A Bear No More	77
CHAPTER FIFTEEN:	Going South	81
CHAPTER SIXTEEN:	California Dreaming	85
CHAPTER SEVENTEEN:	Hockey and Salsa	90
CHAPTER EIGHTEEN:	Hanging Up My Skates	94
CHAPTER NINETEEN:	One More Shift	97
CHAPTER TWENTY:	From Me to You	102

Foreword

When I was asked to make a video introduction for Willie O'Ree for the 1998 NHL All-Star Game celebration in Vancouver for the 40th anniversary of his first game in the National Hockey League, I was truly honored. Just a few years before, when I decided to take up hockey, the first thing I did was look into the history of blacks in hockey. That was how I found out about Willie. What an interesting guy!

Although he is best known for being the first black player in the history of the NHL, Willie O'Ree has become much more than that, quickly developing into one of the greatest ambassadors the sport of hockey has ever known. Each time I read an article on his work as the Director of Youth Development for the NHL/USA Hockey Diversity Task Force program, spreading the hockey gospel, I am proud to call him "friend."

It's nice to see the face of the game changing. Boys and girls of all backgrounds are playing this game. Because of Willie's hard work, my sons, Spencer and Mason, are more likely to have teammates that look like them. But Willie's message is not just hockey, it's a message of life, fair play, education, and of sportsmanship.

And that's why we have guys like Grant Fuhr, Anson Carter, Mike Grier, Peter Worrell, Kevin Weekes, and so many others in the league. Willie blazed the trail for everyone who came after him. It just amazes me that he is still out there, conducting clinics, speaking at school gatherings, visiting hospitals, and advising parents, coaches, youngsters, and administrators alike.

Through his sheer perseverance, Willie has created, and continues to create hockey history.

*** Cuba Gooding, Jr.***

CHAPTER ONE

THE FIRST STEP FORWARD

My life in hockey goes back a long way, more than 60 years, in fact, to a cold winter day in 1938 in Fredericton, New Brunswick, when I first stepped onto the ice. Ever since then, the ice has been a place where I could go faster than I ever could go on land, so fast sometimes that it seemed as if I was flying. There on those outdoor rinks with nothing but ice under me and a crisp blue winter sky above me, it sometimes seemed as if I was the ruler of the whole world and the ice was mine alone. This was not surprising, really, because even though I was often flying flat on my backside, the ice really *was* my own.

Like so many other Canadian boys and girls, I learned to skate in my own backyard. We had a nice big yard, good for end-to-end rushes. When my dad flooded it that winter long ago, I had my own instant ice rink. It was the best present a three-year-old could ever get.

Since I was so young, I didn't have real skates. Instead, I had a kind of beginner's skates, which were very common at the time: two blocks of wood, each with two metal blades on the bottom. There were two leather straps attached to the blocks of wood. The double blades acted the same way that training wheels do on bikes. My dad looped them over my shoes, tightened them up, then sent me out on the ice.

It was kind of like learning to swim by having someone toss you into the deep end of a pool. My dad and eldest brother Richard watched over me, but I taught myself to skate. I pushed an old chair in front of me for balance, and

I took my fair share of tumbles. Soon, though, my movements became bolder, and I learned how to glide. Then my dad gave me a hockey stick, and I learned that this was much better for balance than any chair. Once I had a puck on the end of that stick, I wanted to become the best skater that I could be. I knew that if I could skate, I could play hockey.

Winter is long in New Brunswick. It comes in November and hangs around until March, so the outdoor skating season is a long one. The frozen ponds, creeks, and rivers of Fredericton became my ice rinks. By the time I was five, I was skating every day, even when it was snowing. We'd take a shovel, clear off the snow, and just skate. If it snowed while we were skating, we'd take a break, clear the rink, and then skate some more. Mother Nature couldn't stop us unless she hit us with a blizzard. Even then, it had to be pretty bad to keep me off the ice.

One of my favorite things to do in winter was to skate to school. I'd skate right along the road and sidewalks of town. The city, as cold cities still do, would put salt down on the pavement to melt the ice. (Salt lowers the freezing temperature of water and will make the ice melt — even though the outdoor temperature remains constant.) Still, I'd always find enough room to skate. As soon as I'd get to school, I would count the hours until I could put my skates back on and speed back along the streets of Fredericton.

When I was playing professional hockey, people used to always say that I was a "natural" skater. This means that my skating speed and control on the ice were a gift from God. It's true. I am blessed with natural athletic ability, but it wasn't something I took for granted. I kept that skating gift polished every day, so that it wouldn't rust.

The First Step Forward

Even as a five year old I was not just skating every day, I was actually playing hockey with my brothers and other neighborhood kids. The game just thrilled me. I had to keep skating, and I had to play hockey. I loved the feel of the wind rushing by as I flew along the ice. I loved the sound of spraying ice chips when I hit the brakes and spun around to charge back the other way. I loved having the puck on my stick and learning how to stickhandle. The speed that I could reach on my skates when I was stickhandling with the puck was like defying gravity. You could zigzag through the other players who tried to take the puck away from you, pulling it back as you sped forward, moving it sideways as they lunged in to take it. And then, just before a hip check or body check smashed you into a snowbank, you could beat them by passing the puck off to a teammate. Or better still, by firing it at the net (which, in our case, was often a pair of rocks as goalposts, with nothing but air behind them).

As anyone who plays the game knows, hockey is about much more than stickhandling. You also have to learn to play without the puck, so you have to learn the defensive game. This means playing in your own end and backchecking. Since hockey is a highly physical sport, you know you're going to hit and get hit, so I prepared myself. It didn't bother me to get hit, and you have to remember that in those days we didn't have helmets, or visors, or mouthguards. Since we were all at risk, we didn't hit other players to injure them. It was rare that anyone got hurt by a good clean check.

It wasn't a case of wanting to play hockey, I *needed* to play. I needed to play because being out there on the ice made me feel more alive than anything else. Hockey was like my oxygen. I had no idea when I was five and six years old that one day I would be playing in the NHL. And the thought that I would break the color barrier wasn't even one that I had, since I didn't know what a color barrier was.

All my friends were white because there were only two black families in Fredericton. The fact that I was black never came up when we played as kids. You could have been purple with a green stripe down the middle of your forehead, and it wouldn't have mattered. It was only later, when I became older, that I learned what "color barrier" meant.

Even though I would become a type of pioneer by being the first black man to play in the NHL in 1958, I learned that black people had played hockey for a long time before that. In Canada's Maritime Provinces (my home province of New Brunswick, along with Prince Edward Island, Nova Scotia, and Newfoundland — all provinces bordered or surrounded by the Atlantic Ocean), there had been large black populations over the years. There were the slaves imported to the "New World" from Africa in the 18th and 19th centuries. There were people who migrated north during the American War of Independence in the 1770s. And there were those who escaped slavery during the US Civil War in the 1860s.

There were black hockey leagues at the beginning of the 20th century. They were called "Colored Leagues" because that was an acceptable term for black people at the time. Teams made up entirely of black players used to draw huge crowds of white people who would come out and cheer them on. Newspapers covered these games, and the reporters said the black players were as good as players in the white leagues. But the blacks and the whites didn't play together in the Maritimes, even though black players like

The First Step Forward

Hipple "Hippo" Galloway and Charley Lightfoot were playing on white teams in the province of Ontario at the same time.

All of my knowledge about color and racism was to come much later in both the game of hockey and of life. When I was a little boy, all I knew was that hockey WAS my life, and that "black" meant the puck, and "white" meant the ice. The only color that mattered then was silver because we all wanted to win the Stanley Cup, and we won it a thousand times on those rinks of childhood. But even if you don't come within a million miles of winning the Cup, the game is so great and so beautiful.

And winning the Stanley Cup is not why I love hockey or why I played the game. I played hockey because I couldn't imagine what life would be like if I didn't. Or maybe I could, and I didn't want to have anything to do with a world without hockey. Hockey was the reason I was put on the earth, and no person, thing, creed, or color was going to stop me from playing it. Hockey would take me far from home and onto the brightest professional stage the game knows. It would give me a home, feed my family, and win me friends. It would give me some of my happiest — and saddest — moments. Most importantly, it made me proud of who I am and what I do. And it made my dreams come true.

CHAPTER TWO

HOME

If I have had an exceptional life so far, you might say it's because I had an exceptional childhood. On one hand, it was a classic Canadian boyhood; on the other, it was as unique as our family was.

The O'Rees were one of the most prominent families in Fredericton. We were good at sports, so a lot of people knew us. We were also one of only two black families living within the city boundaries of Fredericton. You might say that made us stand out a bit.

If you travel northeast from New York City 521 miles, (838 kilometers) you will eventually come to Fredericton, the capital city of New Brunswick, Canada's third smallest province. Today, over 700,000 people live in New Brunswick — an area that's a bit bigger than the states of New Jersey, Massachusetts, Connecticut, and Maryland combined. Yet those states together have a population of 18.5 million people!

There's a lot of room in New Brunswick, and when I was a boy there was even more of it. Then, Fredericton only had 35,000 people. That's not many people for the capital city of a province that became part of Canada when the country was founded, on July 1, 1867. And almost all of those people were white.

The O'Rees lived in a maroon-shingled two-storey house at 245 Charlotte Street. Across the street from us lived the Lawrences, who were the *other* black family in Fredericton. It was a nice street, with lots of deciduous trees lining the road. The trees turned bright colors in the fall and gave lots of leafy shade in the hot summer.

When you walked into our house (which we rented), you would enter the living room. If you went up the stairs, you'd come to the bedrooms and bathroom. If, instead, you kept walking straight back, you would pass through the dining room, the kitchen, and the utility room. And then you would be outside, in the yard where I learned to skate.

We had a huge garden, and in summer we'd grow corn, tomatoes, rhubarb, cucumbers, onions, lettuce — you name it. If I had a baseball practice, I had to make sure that I got my gardening jobs done before I went to play ball. My special job was weeding the garden, and there was no end to the weeds! That's another reason why I loved winter so much. Not only was I able to play hockey every day, but I didn't have to weed that garden!

We also had a henhouse, where we kept chickens for eggs and for meat. Chicken was my favorite meal, and I used to help my dad slaughter the chickens when we needed one for Sunday dinner. Killing chickens didn't bother me. The biggest challenge was just catching the chicken because they can run when they want to. When you caught one, you put the chicken's head on the chopping block, you took the ax, and — kaboom! — the chicken didn't have a head anymore. It sounds hard, but it's the cleanest way to kill a chicken.

Afterwards, we'd dunk the chicken in a pot of boiling water to loosen the feathers for plucking. My dad would take care of the rest, like taking out the liver and heart and stuff before my mom cooked the chicken. You sure learn about life when you kill your own food.

Every Saturday night, my mom would make a big pot of brown beans and bake brown bread. She also used to make boiled cabbage and corned beef, and my dad loved baked pork chops. I would eat whatever was on the table. I had an athlete's appetite, but I can't remember ever being hungry.

On Saturdays in winter, all I wanted to do was get dinner inside me so I could listen to the hockey game on the radio. I was dying to hear what my hero Maurice "Rocket" Richard was doing for the Montreal Canadiens. Since TV didn't exist when I was young, the radio was our only choice. Today things are so dominated by TV that people forget how visual the radio can be. The announcer has to paint word pictures so you can see what he sees.

The expert voice of commentator Foster Hewitt — which would crackle when he got excited or rise when he had to shout over the roaring crowd — kept me glued to that radio. Hewitt created such exciting pictures of the "Rocket" shaking off a checker as he blazed in on some poor goalie that those games seemed as if they were right out back, in the rink in our yard.

Born on October 15, 1935, I was the youngest of 13 children, but my mother had two sets of twins who died on her — one in childbirth, the other, shortly after they were born. By today's standards, we had a huge family, but in those days families were large. People wanted a lot of kids around to look after them in their old age. My oldest sister Violet was 21 when I was born, and my eldest brother Richard was 13, so they were almost like an aunt and uncle to me when I was growing up. The rest of us were jammed in between: Thelma, Alfred, Margaret, Lewis, Robert, Betty, who was two years older than me, and then the baby, which was me.

My dad, Harry Douglas O'Ree, worked for the city engineering department, supervising the construction of roads in the summer and snow removal in the winter. He worked 38 years for the city, a length of time which is not common today. Most people are lucky to stay in a job for 10 years, let alone nearly 40. I played pro hockey for 20 years, so I was lucky, too.

My dad was a relatively small man, about 135 pounds soaking wet, but he was strong and wiry. My mom, who was born Rosebud Wright, weighed about 150 pounds and had a big, ready smile. My dad loved baseball, and he used to play it, so I learned to love it, too. My mom didn't play, but she was always interested in what we were up to. My sister Betty played basketball and ran track, and I played hockey, baseball, basketball, tennis, and volleyball. I also swam and played on the championship rugby team. If there was something around, I just played it. Then I narrowed it down to hockey and baseball, with hockey coming first.

Thinking about it all now, I guess I was closer to my mom than to my dad. I spent so much time around her because we were the last two kids at home. My mom ran the household as far as curfews and stuff went. If she said be home at 10 o'clock, you were home at 10 o'clock, not a minute later. If I didn't show up on time, I'd be grounded and have to stay in on weekends. I said to myself, if these are the rules, I'd better obey them. Even though I was the baby, my mom made sure I didn't take advantage of her. My sister Betty, who was a couple of years older than me, got away with much more than I did. Or maybe it just seemed that way.

By the time I was 10, there was just my sister Betty and me living at home. My sisters were all married, Richard was married, Robert and Lewis were living away, and Alfred had passed away in 1949. There was no big crush to get into the bathroom in the morning. It wouldn't have bothered me anyway since I was always an early riser because of hockey. I'm still like that. If I set my alarm for 5:30 AM, I'll wake up at 5:15, and that's it. Once I'm awake, I'm up and at my day. I've always said it's better to be an hour early than two minutes late.

My grandparents from both my parents' sides lived in Gagetown, a small community outside of Fredericton, where a lot of black families lived. The Saint John River runs through Fredericton, and outside of town is a place called Barker's Point, which was also home to mainly black people. Spring Hill was black as well. So even though the O'Rees were one of the only two black families in town, there were other black people living nearby. My brother Richard lived in Barker's Point, and we had friends in Spring Hill. We'd go up to see them and play cards, or they'd come down to see us.

Fredericton was a friendly place then, and fun was fun. You didn't have to lock your doors at night, and people trusted each other. Now it seems that everyone is scared of what a neighbor might do, but back then life just seemed wonderful. Sure there was prejudice, but my parents warned me that there would be, so it wasn't a surprise to find it close to home. Even so, nobody in Fredericton ever told me that I couldn't do something just because the color of my skin wasn't white. And my parents made it clear to me that I could do whatever I wanted, as long as I was true to the way they raised me — to be a good person.

In the end, the way they raised me allowed me to help them. The mother of the other black family in town, Mrs. Isabell Lawrence, was great friends with my mom. My mother always loved her house, and one day, after her boys had moved away, Mrs. Lawrence told my mom that her house was up for sale.

It was 1952, and I was away playing junior hockey in Quebec, and word came that Mrs. Lawrence wanted to sell

Home

the house and land for $3,000. I was getting $60 a week to play junior hockey, which was pretty good money for the time. I'd been keeping pocket money and sending the rest to my mother, which we kept in a joint account. There was money in the bank to buy the house, and I said to my parents, "Go get a real estate agent, and let's do it."

They did, and we bought the house. Mrs. Lawrence must have felt her time on earth was nearing its end, because by the time we had moved into the house, she was dead. To this day I don't know why she didn't leave it to her sons, but she just loved my mother. Mom used to cook for her, and I used to shovel her driveway and clean snow off her steps, and maybe she just wanted us to have a house of our own.

We moved in and fixed up the house, which was smaller than the one we had been living in across the street. We had a cellar downstairs, and that's where my mom would bottle vegetables because it was cool. It was such a relief to my mom and dad to know they were in their own house and it was all paid for. That's one of the things I was proudest of — hockey gave me money to send to my parents to help them buy a house. They had always made a home for me, a wonderful place that I would go back to in a second if I could time travel. And because of hockey, I could help make a home for them. It makes me proud still.

CHAPTER THREE

SCHOOL DAYS

Today, because of my job, I spend a lot of time in schools. Fortunately, I loved school, so going back inside to talk about my life and work doesn't make me nervous. I think it might have made me nervous if I had been a bad student.

I'm not saying I was perfect, and I'll tell you about a couple of things that I did when I was a kid to prove that I wasn't. All I'm saying is that your school days are a time when you're free to learn everything you can, without having to worry about finding a job or earning a living. With all the resources available to you today, like the Internet, videos, and CD-ROMs, the world has become very small. I sometimes wish I was back at school, so I could plunge into all the wonderful ways there are to learn. I don't even think I'd mind taking a test again. Well, maybe I'd mind a spelling test.

I went to two elementary schools in Fredericton. From grades one through six, I went to Smythe Street School. It was just two-and-a-half blocks from my house, so I had no excuse for being late. Then, because of some change in the school zoning laws, I went to York Street School, which was also two-and-a-half blocks away, but in the other direction. I went there for grades seven and eight. Both of them are closed now, and York Street School has been converted into a cultural center.

Since I loved going to school, I liked having homework. It made me feel connected to school. My favorite subjects were social studies and arithmetic — or math, as you'd call it today — because I was good at them. I guess you also have to have problems with one subject, and I wasn't so good at spelling.

I would do anything to try to miss those spelling tests. I'd say that I had lost my spelling book in a snowbank and had to wait for the spring thaw before I could find it again. Or that the tuna fish sandwich that I had for lunch was acting kind of funny in my stomach and might decide to come up for air in the middle of the test, so that I'd better leave for the sake of decency. Sooner or later, though, I'd have to take the spelling test. English is a funny language: every time you learn a spelling rule, you also have to learn an exception to that rule. "I before E except after C," and so on. There weren't any computers to fix things for you.

Even though World War II was going on when I started school, it didn't trouble my childhood. Canadians and Americans (my brother Lewis was in the merchant marine) were off fighting the Germans, but we went on as if everything was normal. Sometimes at recess we'd play soldiers, but mainly we'd play baseball or basketball. I loved recess, and I loved phys ed class because it seemed like recess.

My favorite teacher was Mrs. Smith, who taught me in grade three. She was a very nice lady, very motherly towards us, and she loved teaching. It's easy to spot a teacher who loves their work — they're as sorry to see the class end as you are.

I also remember a couple of principals, Mr. Close and Mr. Clowater, but that's because I got sent to their offices — not often, but when I was, it wasn't pleasant. Today in school, kids resolve problem behaviour in discussion groups with their peers, but when I was at school, problems were resolved in the principal's office. I was sent to the principal's office once for leaving the playground without permission, another time for fighting back against bullies, and another time for making jokes in the classroom. When you went to the principal's office, you went to get the strap — a big, tough piece of leather that the principal would whack down on your hand. I would try to pull my hand back just before the strap hit, so the principal would have to do it again. If the offense was serious enough, they'd strap you twice. It hurt, and afterwards the principal wouldn't try to shake your throbbing hand to show what a good fellow he was. He'd just say, "Get out of here, and I don't want to see you back in here again." I'd be thinking exactly the same thing, and I'd get out of there.

I had lots of friends when I was a kid, and I still have some of them. I was very close to the George family. I played on the championship rugby team in high school with Tony and Eddie in 1953. I hung out with Tony, Eddie, and their brothers Louie and Joey — they were like family. Tony, Louie and Joey still live in Fredericton. Eddie moved to Houston. Two other close childhood friends of mine are Walter "Bubsy" Mills who also played rugby with me and John "Jr." Doherty — my fishing buddy. My friends Gus and Johnnie Mazzuca still live in Fredericton and I see them when I go back home in summer. Gus went to St. Dunston's, the Catholic school in town, and I used to go down there and play basketball. My best friend at school was Mike Closter, who was the son of the Anglican minister. Mike was a good-looking kid with sandy hair and an athletic build. His dad's church, St. Anne's, was right at the corner of my street. Mike and I chummed around from the time we were six or seven. We played baseball and ran track and just hung out.

You wouldn't have known Mike was a minister's kid, even though we both sang in the St. Anne's choir and did it for four years. I used to go to church every Sunday. My mom would go, too, though sometimes I'd have to drag my dad. There were two services, one at 8 AM and one at 11. Usually I'd sing in the choir at 11, though I didn't always sing in key.

I was also an altar boy, and every Sunday I would put on the black gown called a cassock, and then the white lacy top, called a surplice, over it. I often carried the cross down the aisle to start the service. Everyone would be looking at me, and I'd be trying not to look back. It was fun being an altar boy.

Sometimes Mike and I would go to church and sit in the back pew and kind of giggle during the service. Mike's father would give us heck. Not only was it bad manners for the minister's son to be laughing during church, it was just as bad that we were laughing while Mike's dad was trying to work.

The craziest thing that Mike and I ever did was when I was 10 or 11. We went out right in front of his house, and we lay down on the road. I was laying with my hands back behind my head, just relaxing, and cars were honking at us like mad. The minister, Mike's dad, came flying out of the house when he heard all the noise. "What the H," and he meant Hell, "are you kids doing?" he shouted, and we explained it all to him. We were lying in the middle of a busy road because we wanted to know what it felt like to be dead. Even the minister had to laugh at that one.

That road figured into my life the only time the police ever came. We used to play baseball in the middle of the road, and even though we didn't break any windows, the neighbors complained. For some reason, they didn't like kids. So they called the police, and the police came, and we hid. When they had gone, we'd come out and play ball again, and the police would come back. They told us we had to stop playing ball because there were complaints. We were quite bold in telling them that there was only one complaint, from this one family, and we wanted to complain about them. They didn't like us just because we were kids. The police laughed and said, for the time being, we should play down at the park.

The one time the police should have been called, they weren't. There used to be this old guy named Sam who traveled the streets of Fredericton buying beer bottles. The big ones were worth three cents, and the little ones were worth a penny. Sam had a horse and a red wagon and a bell, and you'd see him coming. My friends and I would get some bottles, we'd hail Sam, and he would get down from his wagon.

While some of us were selling him the bottles, the others would run around behind his wagon and steal some of his bottles. He wouldn't see a thing, and he'd give us our money and drive off. Then we'd dash over to the next block and hail him again, and sell him back his own bottles. It seems a terrible thing to have done now, but we were just having fun and making a bit of money.

I didn't have any girlfriends because there weren't that many black girls at school. It wasn't done for a black boy to be seen with a white girl, and my parents had always said, "Stick to your own kind" to avoid trouble. I had crushes on girls who played sports, but I kept them to myself. I didn't take girls to the movies, but I'd go with my friends.

There were two theaters: the Capitol at the corner of Regent and King, and the Gaiety on Queen Street. The Capitol played Westerns, the Gaiety showed more love stories, so we always went to the Capitol. I loved Westerns. It cost a dime to see a movie and a nickel for popcorn, so you could see a double feature for a quarter. My favorites were *The Durango Kid* and *Red Rider* and the *Little Beaver* series. I still love Westerns and watch them as often as I can on TV or on video. My wife says to me, "But you've seen that movie a dozen times!" and I say that I don't care. It's as good as it ever was.

All in all, my school days were some of the happiest times of my life. In 1998, I went back to Fredericton to make a presentation at Fredericton High, my old high school. It was wonderful walking down the halls that I knew so well and standing there in the auditorium at the assembly, speaking to the kids. I hadn't been back there since 1954, and it brought back a lot of memories. A lot of good memories. That's the thing I say to kids about school, that either way you're going to remember it, so you might as well make those memories good ones.

CHAPTER FOUR
GONE FISHING

Everyone needs a place to escape to. I mean the kind of place that takes you right outside your life. The kind of place where you can look beyond yourself into the bigger world. For me, that place is called Island Lake north of Fredericton, and I've been going there ever since I was a boy.

Island Lake is really several lakes, and they're in my home province of New Brunswick. I used to go out there on weekends and in summer with my brothers and my friends. Now I still go there in summer, with friends, to fish and relax and think about life. Every year, I look forward to these trips. I know that just being in the crisp clean air, with the evergreen trees thick on the banks of the lake, and the fish leaping in the cool blue water, will make me happy. It fuels me up for the rest of the year.

When the snows left each year, my brother Richard, his son Dougie, some friends, and I would hike to Island Lake. We'd bring camping gear and our fishing rods, and we'd set up camp over a weekend during the school year, or longer in summer. You have to remember that there weren't any convenience stores on Island Lake, there weren't any hotels, there wasn't even any electricity or plumbing. There was just you, your wits, and the great outdoors. Going to Island Lake taught me a lot and helped me prepare for a life in hockey.

At Island Lake I learned how to look after myself. If you didn't catch any fish, then you were going to go hungry. If you didn't find fresh water, then you were going to be thirsty. And if you didn't make your camp properly, then

Gone Fishing

you were going to be dinner for the insects, not to mention at the mercy of the wind and the rain.

Of course, my brother and friends weren't going to let me starve, and I'd learned a few things in the Cub Scouts and the Boy Scouts. But out there on Island Lake, I learned teamwork by looking out for my companions as much as they were looking out for me. We were all in this great adventure, and what was good for one was good for all.

We'd have competitions to see who could catch the biggest trout, and we'd always throw back the little ones. It got a little nerve-racking at the end of the day if we hadn't caught much, but somebody always managed to pull a big enough trout out of that lake to feed us.

Then we'd build a campfire and fry the trout up in a bit of butter in a frying pan. We'd roast potatoes that we'd brought along, and we'd have sodas, and it would be a regular feast. Then as the sun went down, we'd talk about life. Out there in the great open country, after a day of fishing, it felt as if there wasn't anything that you couldn't do. And at night, with a million stars stretching off forever into that black sky, I understood what people meant when they said, "The sky is the limit." It didn't seem as if there were any limits, and I would think about what I wanted to do in the coming weeks or years. It was out there on Island Lake that I saw myself as a pro hockey player, even though hockey was miles away.

My brother Richard is dead now, and before he died, he asked me to go back to Island Lake one last time for him to check out the fishing. I did, and it was emotional. It brought back a lot of memories. In fact, I just went back again to Island Lake. The fishing is great. When I was a kid you could bring out as many trout as you wanted, but now you're only allowed five, in order to preserve the stock. They've modernized the place a lot. They've got showers, washrooms, cooking camps, and sleeping camps. I must say that I'm glad about the showers and washrooms.

On the bank of the lake, you'll still see moose, deer, and beaver. And it's just so peaceful. Every time I think of it, I just get the shivers. I can feel the rod and the trout hitting the line, and because I have fished all my life, it's something that I get excited about. There's a whole lifetime of memories at Island Lake. It's the memories that helped me put my life in perspective. Whenever something was getting me down, I'd say, "There's always Island Lake to go back to." You need that in your life. You always need something to look forward to. And when I was a boy, I was looking forward to a life in hockey. Out there on Island Lake I dreamed that I was skating in the big leagues. Soon that dream would come true.

CHAPTER FIVE

MY STAR STARTS TO RISE

By the time I was five years old, I had graduated from my double-runner skates to real ones. Then when I could skate well enough on real skates, I began to play in my first organized hockey league.

I lived in the west end of Fredericton, and we played at Wilmont Park. I still remember my first jersey — it was orange and black, like a tiger. Kids today play inside in nice rinks with all the comforts that the pros enjoy. When I started playing organized hockey, we didn't even have benches. We just had an outdoor rink, with boards around it. Sometimes the snow would be piled up so high around the boards that people just stood on snowbanks, looking down at us as we played. I didn't play in my first indoor rink until I was 15!

The kind of hockey we played was more like shinny — that's a loose kind of hockey that you still see played on ponds, or on asphalt with roller blades. We didn't have any blue lines painted on the ice, nor did we have any face-off circles. We just had a red dot painted where the puck should be dropped. This was not the end of the world, since hockey had only been using the blue line since 1918, and the red line wasn't introduced until 1943.

Sometimes it would start snowing during a game, and we'd stop and sweep off the rink. Sometimes we had to call games off because of the snow, but not too often. I was a left-handed shot and played left wing throughout my early career. First I played pee-wee, or what they call squirts and mites today. Then I played bantam, then midget, then junior.

I was always ready to play hockey when I was a kid, and my routine didn't change too much. We usually had Saturday morning games, so I'd have a little breakfast — nothing too much in my stomach because I didn't want to be too weighed down. I'd put on all my gear at home except for my skates because we didn't have any locker rooms at the outdoor rink. We didn't even have sheds you could get warm in!

My gear was pretty simple. I had shin guards, a protective cup, hockey pants, elbow pads, shoulder pads, a stick, and gloves. Equipment is much better today. It's lighter and tougher, and it fits the contours of your body much more closely, so it gives more protection. I still have my equipment from the last year I played pro, but compared to the gear of today, it seems prehistoric.

Before I'd go to play, my parents would tell me to be careful because they didn't want me to get hurt. I'd always be ready, and I'd do a warm-up on the ice to stretch my muscles. My parents weren't so lucky and had to bounce up and down on the sidelines to keep warm as they watched me play. They used to come to all my games, even when I was a little guy. It's good to have someone cheering you on when you play, and I used to play extra hard for my parents. We didn't practice all that much when I was a kid. Sometimes we'd have an evening practice, but we did most of our practicing in games. There was no hanging around talking about the game afterward, either. It was too cold! We'd just all pile into our parents' cars and head for home. I'd have a shower, wash my underwear, and hang up my shoulder pads, just waiting for the next game.

When I was in my teens, I played with my brother Richard, who was in his 20s, and guys who were bigger than me. I could handle myself. On several occasions Richard would body check me hard to the ice, and I'd say, "My

My Star Starts to Rise

goodness, brother, why did you do that?" He'd say, "You're going to get hit, so you'd better learn how to get hit." And I did. Richard was stocky, 5'10" and 215 pounds, and he played defense. He would never use his stick on guys. Instead he would check them cleanly, with his strong body. I was always prepared to take a blow and to give a good clean hit when I saw the chance to do so.

One of those chances came when I was in my first year of high school. I tried out for the school team, and the coach's son was playing on the team. This can sometimes be a problem, and sometimes not, depending on the coach. This time it was a problem. I was on the ice and the coach's son was skating towards me with the puck. He had his head down, and I stepped into him and knocked him down. He broke his collarbone. The coach was very upset about this and didn't want me on the team because he said I was too rough.

I was disappointed, but I went out and found something else. I won a spot on the Fredericton Junior Capitals, who were a high-flying local junior team in the New Brunswick Junior Hockey League. When I was 17, I moved up to the Senior Capitals. With their black and white uniforms, and their fame, it was like playing for the Los Angeles Kings. I couldn't actually get paid playing for the Capitals because it would have ruined my amateur standing at school, so they gave me money for travel and meals when the team was on the road. The funny thing was that once the high-school coach saw me playing with the Capitals, he wanted me to come back to play for the school team. I said no. He'd had his chance, and he didn't want me. I played with the Capitals for two years, and in 1954-55 I went away to play my first year of junior with the Quebec Frontenacs.

In my teens, my athletic ability gave me confidence. I was good at track, rugby, basketball, and soccer, and I was very good at baseball and hockey. I felt like I could do anything I wanted to do. I had confidence not only to say no to the high school coach but to cross my first color barrier.

Even though Fredericton was a pretty tolerant place, there were still places that a black person couldn't go. For instance, a black person couldn't go into a white barbershop to have his hair cut. There weren't signs up or anything like that — we just knew. If I couldn't go into a place because I was black, well, I couldn't go. But it still bothered me.

Five houses down, on the same side of the street where we lived, there was a family called McQuade. I became friends with their son, and Joe, his dad, who was a barber, would cut my hair on his porch. We became very good friends. I used to walk by the shop where he worked, and I'd wave to him, and he waved back. So one day I asked him what would happen if I came into his shop to have him cut my hair. He paused, looked at me, then said, "I don't know. I haven't given it any thought." So I told him I was going to come in for a haircut.

As I mentioned, the O'Ree family was a very prominent family in Fredericton. My sisters were involved in sports, I was involved in sports, and we were very well known. When I walked into Joe McQuade's barbershop, heads turned. The four barber chairs were occupied, and there were a couple of people waiting. I sat down, and Joe nodded at me. When it was my turn, Joe was occupied, and the next barber looked at me suspiciously. I said, "I'm waiting for Mr. McQuade." You could have heard a pin drop. And when Joe was finished with the customer in front of me, he cut my hair. I knew what was going on, but I wasn't nervous, I just sat there. I was 13 years old.

Then I just started going in. I knew that Mr. McQuade got some flak for it, but I kept going and he kept cutting my hair. When he retired, I went back to his house, and he cut my hair there. It may seem like a small thing, but for me it was huge. I was just a teenager, but it showed me that I could change things if I tried. My parents worried that trouble would happen because of color, but I worried trouble *was* happening because of color. I wasn't going to let color stop me. I knew then that I could play hockey with the big guys or get my hair cut in a white barbershop. I also knew that there hadn't yet been a black man who played pro in the NHL. My young eyes were clearly seeing how the world around me worked. Little did I know how precious that sight was.

CHAPTER SIX

GAME OVER?

In the last year of my junior career, my plans to play pro hockey were nearly smashed to bits by a puck. Hockey is a beautiful game, full of creativity and grace, but it's also a dangerous one. When you have a small piece of frozen rubber flying about at top speed, it's possible to get hurt. And I got hurt. So hurt that it looked as if my hockey life was over.

I had wanted to make the big leagues ever since I was 14 and started thinking seriously about my life. I was playing hockey with my older brother Richard, and something just kept going through my mind. I said to myself, "You're playing hockey, you love this sport, you're devoting a lot of time to it." So I asked myself, "What is the goal here?" And my answer was that I just wanted to play professional hockey.

My brother was my first mentor, and even though he was happy playing at home, with people he knew, he wanted me to go out and see the world. "You can do it," he'd tell me, and I knew that I could. I wanted to see the world, too. Richard reminded me that I'd be seeing it from a unique position. "You could be the first black man in the NHL," he said. At first the idea went in one ear and out the other. Then it came back, and I would hear it running through my head. Maybe I could make the NHL.

That's what Phil Watson said, when he asked me to play for the Quebec Frontenacs. Watson had played center and right wing for the New York Rangers and the Montreal Canadiens for 13 seasons, and he had even won the Stanley Cup. "You've got the skills and the ability to play in the NHL, O'Ree," he told me, after seeing me play for the

Game Over?

Fredericton Capitals. He also told me that because of my color, I was going to get a rough time from the other players and the fans.

But he said that if I kept my head and didn't pay attention to them, I could make it. This was thrilling to hear since he was the first coach to say that I could play in the NHL. If anyone knew what it took to play in the NHL, he did. I told my brother Richard. He smiled and said, "I knew that if you applied yourself and focused yourself you could do it."

But I hadn't done it yet. I played a year of junior for Phil in Quebec, then I went to play in Kitchener-Waterloo, for the Junior Canucks, for the 1955-56 season. I was 20 now, and eager to make my way in the game. The coach in Kitchener was another former NHL player, "Black Jack" Stewart. He wasn't really black. That was just his nickname (a blackjack is the club that policemen used for knocking villains on the head). He was tough and built like my brother Richard — stocky and strong. Stewart had won Stanley Cups as a defenseman with Detroit and then played a couple of seasons with Chicago, before becoming a coach. And eventually, he became a member of the Hockey Hall of Fame.

We were in Guelph, Ontario, playing a game, and Stewart put me out on the ice. I chased the puck into the Guelph zone and dug it out. I passed it back to the blue line to my teammate, Kent Douglass (who later played for Toronto). Then I skated to the Guelph net to put some traffic in front of the goalie.

Kent took a slapshot from the point, just as a Guelph defenseman cross-checked me. This spun me around, and I looked over my right shoulder to see where the puck was. Well, the puck had deflected off a stick, and it was headed right for my face. It hit me just above my right eye. It felt as if my head exploded. I dropped down to the ice, which was turning red with my blood.

They loaded me into an ambulance and took me to the hospital. The damage was bad: I had a broken nose, a broken cheekbone, and I was cut. Worse, I couldn't see out of my right eye. They performed surgery and tried to put me back together. The next morning, when I woke up, I had a big patch over my right eye, but I couldn't see out of my left eye either. I knew my right eye was in trouble, but my left eye was like someone had pulled a curtain over it. I was blind! The nurses called it hysterical blindness and said, "You'll get your vision back." I wasn't so sure. I blinked and strained as hard as I could with my left eye, and then a bit of light came in, and then a bit more. You can imagine what a huge relief that was.

But it didn't last long. I was lying there in bed, wondering about my future when the doctor came to see me. His name was Henderson, and I'll never forget this doctor as long as I live because what he said changed my life. He looked at me and said, "Willie, I'm sorry to inform you that the puck did so much damage to your right eye that the retina at the back of your eye is completely shattered." He looked at me lying there, a scared 21-year-old kid in a city where I didn't know anybody. Then he added the final blow: "There's nothing that we can do for you. You'll never play hockey again."

"You'll never play hockey again." How those words rang in my head as I lay in that sterile hospital bed. My family and friends were a thousand miles away, and there was no one to comfort me. My dream of professional hockey was gone. It seemed like the end of the world. "You'll never play hockey again" kept running over and over in my mind. But I had already decided that hockey was going to be my life! Other people, people I respected, thought so, too. How could this doctor know that I would never play hockey again?

When I called my family, I softened the blow a little. I told them that I had been injured, but that it wasn't too bad. My dad said, "Find another job, find something else to do." I could see his point, but I hadn't accomplished my goal, and I wasn't going to quit.

I stayed in the hospital for a couple of days, and then I went home. After about eight weeks my wounds had healed up pretty well, so I said to myself, "I'm going to try skating again." My legs were strong, I could still skate, and I could shoot the puck. The only problem was that I just couldn't see out of my right eye. It was completely black, like I was still wearing an eyepatch. That doctor's words, "You'll never play hockey again," kept nagging at the back of my mind. But I said to myself, "Wait a minute, this doctor doesn't know how I feel inside. He doesn't know what my goals and dreams are. He doesn't know anything about me!" So I decided that since I felt so well, I'd start playing again.

When I first stepped on the ice in a game, I was a little gun-shy, and I'd flinch away when the puck came at me. I told myself that if I kept doing that, it was definitely going to spoil my game. So I decided to go full steam ahead. I could see well enough out of my left eye, and that was good enough for me. My mother and father were totally against my playing hockey. My father said I was taking a terrible chance because if I got hit in my left eye, I'd be completely blind. All my friends said to find another sport.

It's so important to have the proper equipment, especially helmets and face shields. Hockey is a beautiful game, but it's a dangerous one, and in the blink of an eye you can lose your eye.

But I decided to keep playing. I didn't wear any type of face shield; I didn't wear any helmet; I just kept my head up. The more I played, the more confident I became. It wasn't easy, though. I was a left shot, and I was playing left wing, but I had no right eye. This meant that I had to turn my head quite a bit so my left eye could see what was happening. I was having to slow down, and guys who could never touch me before were hitting me now. They knew I'd been hit by the puck, but they didn't know I was blind in my right eye. And that's the way I was going to keep it. As long as I played, no one was ever going to know. It was my secret. But I worried, even if I kept it secret, was my injury going to ruin my career like that doctor said?

I finished my last year of junior hockey and went home to Fredericton. Would my next stop be the pros? Or would it be nothing? I was visiting my sister Thelma, and there was a knock on the door. My sister answered it and called out, "There's a Mr. Imlach here to see you." Mr. Imlach was none other than George "Punch" Imlach, who would go on to be one of the most famous hockey coaches in history.

Back then, he wasn't famous. Even so, he was famous enough for me. He told me that he just happened to be "in the neighborhood," which was amazing, since he was about 1,000 miles out of his own neighborhood! He told me that he wanted to sign me to a contract to a team in Quebec called the Aces. He said that he was putting together "a championship club," and that I was the kind of guy he wanted on his team. He'd give me $3,500 for the year, plus a $500 signing bonus.

That was $4,000 for a guy with one eye, just out of junior! It was great money at the time. Even so, I wasn't going to go so easily. So I said, "Punch, if you're putting together a championship team, that means that we're going to get in the playoffs. I want $300 if we get into the playoffs. And more money if I score 20 goals."

Punch wasn't happy about it, but he gave me more money. So I joined the Aces and began my pro hockey career. In spite of all my fears about my eye, the game was not over at all. But then I got a chance to play pro baseball. What should I do? Leave hockey for the safety of baseball? What game should I play?

CHAPTER SEVEN

PLAY BALL?

If I hadn't been a hockey player, I would have been a baseball player. As I told you, my dad loved baseball, and he was a fine player. I might have picked up some of my gift from him. I played shortstop and second base for Little League teams in Fredericton when I was a boy — and I wasn't too bad with the bat either. I loved hearing the hard sharp crack of the bat striking the ball when you got good wood on it. I loved watching the ball arch out over the fielders. I loved the smells, too: cut grass, oiled leather baseball gloves, wooden bats, and summer. I loved baseball.

In 1949, when I was 13, I played for the West Enders, a ball team that won the bantam city championship of Fredericton. As a reward, we also won a trip to New York City. It was my first trip to the Big Apple, and we drove down there with our sponsors in five or six cars, as excited as could be. We were going to see the Yankees and the Brooklyn Dodgers.

The Yankees were the greatest team in baseball history. They had won the World Series 11 times by 1949 and would win it again that autumn. The likes of Babe Ruth, the "Sultan of Swat," had worn the Yanks' pinstripe blue uniform and made it famous. The Yankees were baseball. But to me, the Brooklyn Dodgers were even greater because they had Jackie Robinson playing for them.

In 1947, Jackie Robinson became the first black man to play major league baseball. He wasn't the first black man to play baseball — the so-called "Negro Leagues" had been in

Play Ball?

existence for decades, and some of the finest baseball in the world was played there. Sadly, the Negro Leagues had to exist because black men were forbidden by prejudice in the United States from playing in the "majors" with white men.

Jackie Robinson changed all that, and Canada helped. Before he made the major league, Jackie played for the Montreal Royals, who were the Brooklyn Dodgers top farm club. People in Montreal just loved him, and he loved them back. He was a first-class player, but people knew he was a first-class person. They were rooting for him. They knew what he was up against.

And he was up against a lot. When he joined the Brooklyn Dodgers in 1947, people said terrible things about him. Pitchers on other teams would aim the ball at his head. Fans would throw things at him. Even worse, one of his own teammates in Brooklyn started a petition demanding that Robinson be kicked off the team! Another time, in the South, Robinson got a death threat before a game from the Ku Klux Klan. The KKK are the bigots who hide behind white hoods. They hate everyone who isn't white and Protestant. And they do more than hate — within my lifetime they have killed people whose crime it was to be born black.

You have to remember that the world in which you've grown up is much better than the one I grew up in. Sure there are problems with drugs and crime, and yes, people still hate and kill each other because of race or religion. But most people today don't care about race or color or ethnic background, and especially not in sport.

Back in 1949 though, Jackie Robinson was a huge role model for someone like me. He was the bravest man in the world for believing in his dream — and for making it happen. We went to Ebbets Field to watch the Dodgers play and meet Jackie Robinson. When he started talking to me, I couldn't believe it. Here was my idol speaking to me! We talked about playing baseball and hockey. Robinson knew all about hockey from his time in Montreal. Then he said to me, "But there are no black men playing hockey."

I shook my head and corrected my hero. "I play hockey, Mr. Robinson. And one day, I'll play in the big leagues, too." And Jackie Robinson smiled at me. I felt like I had won the World Series myself. Though the Yankees would beat Brooklyn for the championship later that year, Jackie Robinson was named the league's Most Valuable Player. I met him later at a banquet when I played in Los Angeles, when I *was* a professional hockey player, just like I told him I would be. I was very proud.

If someone had told me when I first met Jackie Robinson that seven years later I could have a career in big-league baseball, I would have laughed. That's what happened, though. In 1956, I was playing in the summer for the Marysville Royals, a New Brunswick senior baseball team. I played to keep in shape for hockey and to earn a bit of money in the off-season. One of the Milwaukee Braves scouts saw me play, so I got an offer to come and try out for them at their camp in Waycross, Georgia. Waycross is in the southeastern part of the state, close to Florida. It's in what's known as the "Deep South," which in those days was not the most pleasant place for a black man to be.

That wasn't the reason I wanted to stay at home, though. I told the scout, "I don't want to go to baseball camp. I'm enjoying doing what I'm doing here. Besides, I'm going to be a hockey player." The scout was set on it though, and he said, "Willie, we've already arranged it, so why don't you go and see what it's like?"

Play Ball?

So I went. This was the first time I had ever been to the South, and I flew into Atlanta. I walked into the airport terminal, and the first thing that I saw was "White Only" and "Colored Only" washrooms. I couldn't believe it, but since I had to use the washroom, I walked into the colored one. I wasn't going to cause a revolution during my first few minutes in town.

Then I went out of the airport and hailed a cab. I explained to the driver that I needed to stay in Atlanta overnight before going on to Waycross, so he took me to a hotel — an all-black hotel. I had just asked him to recommend a hotel, and he did. A hotel based on race.

The next day, I took the bus to Waycross, and for the first time in my life, I was told to sit at the back of the bus. When we arrived in Waycross, I was assigned a dorm with eight to 10 other ballplayers, guys from the Dominican Republic, the West Indies, and Cuba. Black guys like me. I was getting the picture all too well.

We started training, and the facility was first-class. There were four baseball diamonds at the camp. They had pits in which you could practice sliding, they had pitching pits, and they had great equipment. Still, I kept asking myself, "Why am I here? I don't want to be a professional ballplayer, I want to be a professional hockey player. What happens if I catch on? What am I going to tell them?"

I knew that if the Braves wanted me to stay, I was going to have to turn the contract down and go home. I called my parents. They asked me how I was doing, and I said, "I'm still here." But I didn't want to be. Outside the dorm was a bulletin board, and on it was a list. If your name appeared on this list, it meant you were being sent home. At the end of the first week I went to look, but my name wasn't there, and I was disappointed. This is unusual, I know. Most athletes *want* to make the team. So I asked myself: "Am I really trying my best? Am I really giving 100 percent or just 80 percent?" I decided that since I had come so far, I would try as hard as I could.

But with each day, I knew more and more that I didn't want to be in Georgia any longer than I had to be. Things came to a head that first Sunday when my dorm mates and I left the camp to go to an all-black Baptist church. When we came out of the service, we had 20 minutes to kill, so we looked around. We came to this drugstore, and some of the guys wanted a cold drink because it was hot. I looked to see if there were any signs saying, "Whites Only," but I couldn't see anything. Even so, I hung back by the door, looking at postcards on a rack, while a couple of the other guys went and sat at the soda fountain.

There were these white guys sitting at the soda fountain, and sure enough, they started in with racial remarks and name-calling. So I said, "Come on guys, we better leave," and we got out of there before there was real trouble.

I tried my best in the second week, but my heart wasn't in it. I played in an exhibition game and got a couple of hits, but my name still turned up on the list of people being cut. I went to the office with my head down, as if I was sad. The manager said, "We're impressed with your play, Willie, but you need some more seasoning, so you're going back to New Brunswick." For an athlete, getting cut is supposed to be bad news, but I was as happy as I could be.

But I still had to get out of Georgia and the South. For the first part of the trip home, I had to sit at the back of the bus. The trip home was five days long, so that meant I was at the back for nearly three days. I was only allowed out to use the washroom or grab a sandwich at a rest stop. As we drove farther north, I moved farther up the bus. By the time we got to the Canadian border, I was sitting up front. I was home and knew more than ever the truth of my life: I was going to be a hockey player.

CHAPTER EIGHT

THE DREAM COMES TRUE

My first professional hockey team was the Quebec Aces, in the Quebec Senior Hockey League, in 1956-57. "Professional hockey" doesn't just mean the NHL — there are many leagues where a player can be paid to play, and the Quebec Senior Hockey League was a good one. It had started up after World War II and had teams across the province of Quebec, as well as the Hull-Ottawa Junior Canadiens. The name "Aces" came from fiddling a bit with the initials of the company that owned the team: the Anglo-Canadian Pulp and Paper Company (ACPP). Aces sounded much better than "Acpp," so Aces it was.

As far as the Aces went, you couldn't ask for a better organization. When Punch Imlach showed up at my sister's house and asked me to become an Ace, I was thrilled. Finally, I was going to be a pro hockey player. As I said earlier, I wasn't so starry-eyed that I let them get a bargain. When I did my own contract with Punch and got more money out of him, I wasn't nervous. I didn't think that if I asked for too much he would say, "No, you're too expensive," and walk away. I knew that he would respect me if I asked for what I was worth. And he did. It's a lesson I've taken with me through my life: if you sell yourself cheap, people will treat you cheaply.

Of course, that was a time when $4,000 was good money for a season. In today's terms, that would come out to about $26,000. It didn't cost me much to live in Quebec City, so I'd send money home to my parents to help them out. As I said earlier, it helped them buy a house, and that made me proudest of all.

I had played in Quebec city as a junior, so I knew my way around. I had roomed with a French family and learned the language. I had no problem going into any of the great restaurants in the old part of the city and ordering a meal in French. I could talk to the fans and read what the papers said about us. I even took a business course in French at O'Sullivan Business College. Today, I can still get by in French, but I can write it much better than I speak. As with everything, if you don't use it, you lose it.

Playing for Punch was a treat. People have said that he was a hard guy to get along with. He swore a lot, and he was very superstitious, and some have even said that he was mean, but I can't say enough good things about Punch. He was the type of guy who liked a fast aggressive hockey player, and that was me. I'm really pleased that I had the opportunity to play for him for three years. He was a straight-up kind of guy. If you worked hard, played both ends of the ice, and were aggressive, Punch was the easiest coach in the world to play for. If you didn't, then he could make your life difficult.

That's what made him a champion. He wanted to win, and any player who didn't want to win wasn't going to last long on his team. When Punch went on to coach the Toronto Maple Leafs, his team made the playoffs 10 out of the 11 years that he was the boss of the bench. In four of those years, his team won the Stanley Cup. There was no doubt about it, Punch was a winner.

Punch had also been a player for the Quebec Aces before he became the coach. Before that he had played for Toronto's Bank Leagues (teams would be sponsored by banks and companies), then he moved up to the senior leagues. While he was playing for the Toronto Goodyears in a game in Windsor, he got his nickname. He was knocked down when he was tripped and elbowed, and he whacked his head on the ice. When he came to, he was fighting mad and he took a punch — at his own team's trainer. Some newspaper guy in Toronto wrote that he was "punch-drunk," something that happens to boxers when they get hit on the head too many times. The writer kept calling him Punchy Imlach, and then it just got shortened to Punch.

He wasn't the only fellow who became famous after spending time on the Aces. Three seasons before I arrived, Jean Beliveau left to play for the Montreal Canadiens. Big, graceful Beliveau had been a king in Quebec. As a center, he was without equal, stickhandling the puck through traffic and making perfect passes to teammates. He was handsome, too, and the women loved him. *Everybody* loved Beliveau. Merchants gave him suits and hats and shirts and free steak lunches every time he scored three goals. The Aces gave Beliveau a contract for $20,000 a year, and two cars. One of them was a stylish convertible with the license plate "2 B." The premier of Quebec (who would be like a governor in the US) had the license plate "1B."

Montreal owned Beliveau's NHL rights, but it took them a long time to finally get him to play for them. He was happy in Quebec City and kept saying no. In the end, what the Canadiens did was amazing. They bought the entire Quebec Senior Hockey League! So now they owned the Aces and figured they could make Beliveau do what they wanted. But he went his own way. He'd already decided the time had come to play in the NHL, and he signed on with the Canadiens anyway.

The Dream Comes True

I never got to play with Beliveau, but I sure admired him. He was with the Canadiens for 18 seasons and won the Hart Trophy twice as the NHL's Most Valuable Player. He was also the scoring champion once and the MVP in the playoffs once. He was the Canadiens captain for 10 years and led them to 10 Stanley Cups. He was glorious.

But there was another guy who had played for the Aces who was just as glorious, even though he never made it to the NHL. Herbie Carnegie played for Sherbrooke, another team in the Quebec League. Herbie was black, and he played on an all-black line with his brother, Ossie, and Manny McIntyre, in the 1940s. Herbie Carnegie had grown up in Toronto and played pond hockey there before graduating to bigger teams. Carnegie was a magical stickhandler. The puck seemed to be on a string with him.

And boy, could he make plays! His crisp, seeing-eye passes to McIntyre and brother Ossie made the line the best in the league. He won three Most Valuable Player awards when he played with Sherbrooke and a championship trophy. In the early '50s, he was playing on the Quebec Aces with Jean Beliveau, who was a great admirer of his. It was thrilling for me to sit in the same dressing room that those two giants had sat in.

But the thing about Herbie Carnegie that really interested me was that he never made the NHL. How could a guy who had won not one but *three MVP* awards not be in the big show? Herbie's Jamaican-born dad had warned him when he was a kid that "They won't let any black boys in the National Hockey League."

When Herbie was a teenager, it seemed all too true. His junior team was practicing in Maple Leaf Gardens, where Toronto played their home games, when Conn Smythe saw him. Conn Smythe was the man who invented the Toronto Maple Leafs. He was a complex guy. He was an athlete, a soldier, a pilot, a gambler, and a patriot. He was also a bigot. He more or less didn't trust anyone who wasn't white and Protestant. So even though Smythe saw how good Herbie was, he wouldn't let Herbie play for him. Instead, he said, "I'll give $10,000 to the man who can turn Herbie Carnegie white."

It was an awful thing to say, and Herbie has had to live with this all his life. Smythe was a powerful guy, and the NHL listened to him. Pro hockey could have beaten baseball at breaking the color barrier if the Leafs had signed Herbie, but they didn't.

Things looked like they might change in 1948. Herb Carnegie finally got his shot at the NHL, when he was invited to the New York Rangers' training camp. Even though Carnegie was as good if not better than the best players, the Rangers still wanted him to spend a season on one of their farm teams. Carnegie kept pressing them, and the Rangers said he was an excellent hockey player. In the end, the best they could do was offer him a spot on their top farm team. This is what the Brooklyn Dodgers had done by putting Jackie Robinson on their farm team in Montreal. Maybe the Rangers would have brought Carnegie to the NHL in a year or so, maybe they wouldn't have. We'll never know because Herbie said, "No thanks," and went back to Quebec.

Carnegie and Beliveau were gone from the Aces, and my time was just beginning. I didn't fear the future, I embraced it. In my first season, the team finished in first place with 87 points — which was 13 points better than the second-place team, Chicoutimi. I had a good year — I scored 22 goals and added 12 assists. We made the playoffs and just kept on going. We beat the Brandon Manitoba Regals, and we won the championship for all the minor pro leagues: the Duke of Edinburgh's Trophy. We were the best team in the country.

What a thrill! For me at the time, it was like winning the Stanley Cup. Just a year earlier I had been afraid my career was over. After all, Dr. Henderson had told me that it was. I wondered if he could see me now, holding the championship trophy for the Quebec Aces above my head. I was 21 years old, and I was going places. And one place I knew I was going to get to was that place that had been denied Herbie Carnegie: the NHL.

CHAPTER NINE

BATTLING RACISM

Of course, getting to the NHL was not going to be any easier than getting to the Quebec Aces. In many ways, it was harder. I heard my first racial insult when I was 12 years old. At that age, kids can start taking on the worst traits of adults. Before that, everybody gets along fine. Then you get close to being a teenager, and suddenly everyone becomes nasty, the way grownups are sometimes. But I can tell you, I was never treated as badly by kids as I was by grownups when I played in Quebec.

Don't get me wrong. The fans in Quebec city were great, and I'm not a bitter guy. I don't go around holding grudges. I'm just telling you the way it was, and why it wasn't right, so that you can make sure it doesn't happen to you.

One of my teammates was black, too. His name was Stan Maxwell, and he was from the Maritimes like me. Outside of my brother Richard, Stan was my best buddy. He and I were the only two black guys in the Quebec League, and we were treated like royalty in Quebec City. The problems happened when we went on road trips.

North of Quebec City, there's a small town called Chicoutimi. It's a pretty place on the Saguenay River, but the fans of the Chicoutimi Sagueneens could be ugly. Every time I played in Chicoutimi, I had problems. Stan had played for Chicoutimi, but he's a fair-skinned guy; if you looked at him, you'd think he was white. If you look at me, you know I'm black. And as soon as I hit the ice, I could hear the chants and the name-calling. *"Maudit nègre"* was the most common one. Let's just say that it means something worse than "damned Negro."

I had learned to turn my ears off to that kind of thing. I knew what I was going to be exposed to when I went to other towns. I knew what I was going to hear. And not just from the fans. I had to fight a lot when I first started playing, not because I wanted to, but because I had to. Players would take shots at me that I just couldn't let pass. If I did, then I'd be finished. Everyone would think they could run me.

My parents had told me to turn the other cheek and skate away. I would try to do that, but sometimes I just had to stand up to the bigots and bullies. It bothered me that I had to fight because I felt fighting brought me down to the level of the bullies. I thought that guys who couldn't accept me as just another hockey player had the problem, not me. I said that I was not going to be run out of the league. If I had to leave, it would be because I didn't have the ability, not because of my color.

Now that I think about it, I started fighting when I was 12, when the racial taunts first started. I would say to myself, "I know the type of person I am and I'm not going to let this racial name-calling bother me." But when people keep on taunting you, and then they attack you, you have to fight back. I've had stick fights with guys — terrible ones. But many guys would taunt me, then they wouldn't drop their gloves and fight me honestly. Instead they'd come at me with their sticks, and so I'd have to fight back with mine. That's not sport, that's a type of crime. In my first year with the Aces, I had 80 penalty minutes over 68 games. That was the third-highest total on our team.

It wasn't just the players who came after me because I was black. The fans would attack me, too, and I would chase them into the stands to fight back. The worst place again was in Chicoutimi. Sometimes I'd get a penalty for something or

The Autobiography of Willie O'Ree: Hockey's Black Pioneer

other, and I'd be in the penalty box. Now, in those days, there was no glass between the fans and the players, so if someone wanted to, they could come right down from the stands and step into the penalty box. Not good.

So there I was in the penalty box. I had taken my gloves off to have a drink of water when I heard chanting. It was the usual *"maudit nègre,"* and I figured something was up. The chanting got louder, so I reckoned that someone was coming up behind me to attack me in the penalty box. I didn't turn around; I just waited. When I heard someone step into the penalty box, I spun around and saw this guy who was just about to attack me. Instead, I attacked first and, with one clean punch, sent him flying backwards.

This, as you can imagine, didn't make the fans happy. They started yelling and screaming. Some of them started to climb down towards me in the penalty box. My teammates came to the rescue, and soon we had a real brawl. The guy who tried to attack me got up and tried to escape back up the stairs, but he couldn't because he was blocked by screaming fans. I didn't hurt him because he looked like a scared rabbit. It was ugly, but it certainly wasn't the only time this kind of thing happened.

Sometimes people would spit on me or throw things on me, like drinks. My parents had said life in hockey would be difficult and that the world was filled with racists. I certainly knew it during my time playing in the province of Quebec, and I would know it again, but I wasn't going to quit. I couldn't. Not only did the money I was sending home help my family, I still had my dream. I wasn't going to let a bunch of ignorant, stupid people chase me out of hockey. I was going to show everyone that I could play with the best. And in my second year in Quebec, that chance came.

CHAPTER TEN

THE JACKIE ROBINSON OF HOCKEY

It was Phil Watson, my Quebec Frontenacs junior coach, who first said it to me. He told me that if I applied myself, I had the skills to make the NHL, and if I did that, I could become the "Jackie Robinson of hockey." I had never forgotten that, and now, at age 21, I was ready to prove him right.

In 1957, the Bruins had a "working agreement" with the Quebec Aces. This meant that Boston could invite players in the minor pro leagues to try out for them. It even meant that they could just call up the minor league club and ask for a player to be sent up to the big time. But the NHL was a tough league to get into, no matter what color you were.

You have to remember that there were only six NHL teams at the time. In addition to the Boston Bruins, there were the New York Rangers, Detroit Red Wings, Chicago Black Hawks, Toronto Maple Leafs, and Montreal Canadiens. The NHL was formed in 1917, and there used to be more teams, but they died out due to financial problems. So from 1942 to 1967, there were only six teams who came to be known as the "Original Six."

Since each team carried 21 guys or so, you multiply that by six and you get 126. That's all there was, about 126 jobs for all the guys who wanted to play in the NHL. In 1957, there were 32 teams in the minor pro leagues, and they carried 23 guys each. So if you add those 736 minor league guys to the 126 in the NHL, that means there was roughly

862 guys after 126 jobs. You can see that it was tough to get into the NHL.

In the summer of 1957, I was back in Fredericton, working in a service station, changing oil, pumping gas, that kind of thing. My brother Richard was working for a produce company called Willett Food Company. He'd drive a truck to these small country stores and drop off oranges, potatoes, and apples. The truck was big, what they call a "three-ton truck," and it had a stick shift. Sometimes I'd go with Richard, and he would let me drive on the dirt roads in the country. So my very first vehicle was a three-ton truck. And I still drive a stick shift today, though my vehicle is a lot smaller than that truck.

One day in August, I came home from work, and there was a letter from Boston for me. I picked it up very carefully and looked at the return address. It was from the Boston Bruins. My heart skipped a beat or two as I opened it up. Could this be the letter I had hoped for? Could this be my ticket to the big time?

Not only was it a letter from the Bruins, it was a letter from Lynn Patrick himself. He was the general manager of the team, and he came from hockey's "royal family." Lynn's dad Lester and his uncle, Frank, had been hockey pioneers. They started a league out on Canada's west coast in 1912, with teams in Vancouver, Victoria, and New Westminster. They built the biggest rink in the world in Vancouver — bigger than Madison Square Garden in New York. And since you don't get much ice or snow out on the west coast in winter, the Patricks used artificial ice in their arenas.

Before too long they had teams in Seattle, Washington, and Portland, Oregon. If you ever want to win an easy bet, ask some hockey know-it-all for the name of the first

The Jackie Robinson of Hockey

American team to win the Stanley Cup. I'm sure that they'll tell you it was the New York Rangers in 1928. It wasn't. It was the Seattle Metropolitans in 1917. They were one of the Patricks' teams.

The Patricks also invented the blue line. In early hockey, you couldn't pass the puck forward. You could only pass it sideways, like they pass the ball in rugby. With the invention of the blue line, you then had an offside line. The puck could be passed forward between each team's blue lines, and this made the game more exciting. The Patricks also invented line changes, the penalty shot, the farm-team system, the playoff system, and about two dozen other things, including numbers on jerseys.

Lynn Patrick had played 10 seasons for the New York Rangers at center and left wing, and he had won a Stanley Cup. You could say that getting anything from Lynn Patrick was big deal, but this was better. "Dear Bill," it began (even though no one but strangers called me Bill). "The Boston Bruins will hold their training camp here in Boston at the Boston Garden. We will begin our training period on the afternoon of Sunday, September 15. We would like you to report to the Manger Hotel in Boston before noon on September 15."

I was in heaven. The Bruins training camp! I couldn't wait to show the letter to my parents, and they were thrilled. "You're going to the Bruins training camp, you're going to be playing for the Bruins!" they said. Then my mom asked how many black players were playing in the NHL. "There's none," I told her. "I could be the first." She thought about this, and then very gently said, "We hope it happens, but you've got to think of the worst." That was just like them, worrying that there would be some mistake because I was black. There was no mistake. I framed that letter and I have it still. I was going to be a Boston Bruin.

To tell you the truth, I wasn't thinking of playing for the Bruins at the time because I'd signed a two-year contract with the Quebec Aces. This career development occurred faster than I had planned. I was wondering what my teammate Stan Maxwell would make of all this. When I called to tell him the good news, he had some of his own. He had received a letter, too.

So Stan and I took the train down to Boston. I had never been there before, and I immediately liked the city. It had loads of history because it was so important before, during, and after the American War of Independence. It also had a European feel to it, with its brick buildings and green spaces. I thought that I could be happy playing here.

But first I had to get through training camp. Just stepping onto the ice at Boston Garden was a dream come true for myself and Stan. There we were, two black guys at one of the great NHL rinks. Up on the rafters were the three Stanley Cup banners from 1929, 1939, and 1941. The ice had seen the likes of Eddie Shore, Dit Clapper, Frank Fredrickson, Woody Dumart, and Milt Schmidt skate on it. You probably don't know who these guys are, but if you ever go to the Hockey Hall of Fame in Toronto, look them up because they're all members. And it's even harder to get elected to the Hockey Hall of Fame than it is to make the NHL.

At the time, though, I was thinking more about the current Bruins team than I was about the glory teams of the past. Some NHL teams had one training camp for rookies and another for veteran players, but not Boston. We were all there together, new guys like me and established stars like Doug Mohns, Don McKenney (the nicest guy I ever played with, who was always giving me encouragement), Fleming Mackell, Allan Stanley, Leo Boivin, Vic Stasiuk, Johnny Bucyk, and Jerry Toppazzini.

The established players were great. They treated Stan and me as if we belonged, and it sure made life easier. At some training camps, the rookies are just one thing: a target. Guys try to run them out of the rink because the rookies are looked upon as thieves. They're younger, and they're trying to steal the jobs of the older guys. But it wasn't like that in Boston in 1957. We were like brothers.

We all stayed at the same hotel, and we worked out twice a day. I don't want to sound like I was playing in the Stone Age, but back then training camp was a lot different than it is now. Today, teams have serious weight-training rooms, with nothing but the best equipment. They have strength-testing machines, and stationary bikes, which you can adjust so it feels as if you're riding up and down the Rocky Mountains. They have stereo systems piping in whatever music you want. They have TVs connected to satellite dishes, so you can watch any game, anywhere. They have hot tubs, and cold tubs, and oxygen chambers to speed up the healing of injuries. In fact, some of their rooms for looking after injuries would make hospitals jealous, they're so well-stocked.

Back in 1957, we had no such luxury. The weight room consisted of a set of scales, a couple of whirlpool tubs that looked like giant bathtubs, a couple of stationary bikes, and a table for you to lay on when you got a rubdown. So what we did to train was a lot of skating and a lot of calisthenics. We'd do sit-ups and push-ups on the ice. Our conditioning came from skating and those exercises. I was in pretty good shape, though, because I had been playing baseball at home and working out. While I was at the Bruins camp, I just had to work on getting my lungs used to the strain of skating fast and hard for short periods of time.

Camp lasted a couple of weeks, and at the end of it, I was cut. Coach Milt Schmidt and Lynn Patrick told me that both Stan and I had to have "a little more seasoning." This was what teams said when they wanted you to go back home and get a few more knocks or a bit more maturity. I was disappointed, but I felt that I had shown my stuff to the Bruins. They knew what I could do, so Stan and I figured if we went home and worked hard, maybe we'd have a chance to come back.

I didn't have to wait long. I was back playing for the Quebec Aces, and out of the blue they got a phone call in January 1958. It was from the Bruins, and they said, "We need Willie O'Ree to come up for a couple of games. Tell him to meet the team in Montreal."

I knew from the beginning that I wasn't going to be up for long because the Bruins had an injured player who would return to the lineup. Even so, my time had finally come. I was going to play in the NHL!

I took the train to Montreal and met the team at the Forum. I knew the Forum well because I had been playing there for two years with the Quebec Aces. Just the week before we played against the Montreal Royals there. It was funny — only a day ago I was Willie O'Ree, Quebec Ace. Now I was Willie O'Ree, Boston Bruin.

The Montreal Forum seemed different. The lights were brighter, and the ice was whiter. The fans seemed more elegant, and no one called me any names. I can't properly describe the thrill of pulling on that brown and gold jersey, with the big "B" on the front. Let's just say I was the hap-

The Jackie Robinson of Hockey

piest guy on Earth. It was January 18, 1958, and it was a Saturday. That's *Hockey Night in Canada* night — the biggest hockey night of the week. And we came out flying.

The Montreal Canadiens were in the middle of their five-consecutive Stanley Cups run, and playing them was like playing the Hockey Hall of Fame. I'm on the ice, and suddenly I'm up against my hero, Maurice "Rocket" Richard. Then I see Jean Beliveau, the former star of the Quebec Aces. Or the Rocket's little brother, Henri Richard. Then I'm skating in on goal, and who am I looking at but Jacques Plante, one of the greatest goalies of all time. But first I have to get past Doug Harvey on defense, who some say was the best defenseman to ever lace up skates. I won't argue with them.

Even so, we were the hot team that night and beat the Canadiens 3-0. Montreal only lost 17 games that season and would go on to win the 1958 Stanley Cup, but they couldn't beat us. I didn't get any goals, but I had already accomplished my biggest one. On the night of January 18, 1958, I became the first black man to play in the NHL. Nothing was made of it in the papers or on the radio and TV. Nobody called me the "Jackie Robinson of Hockey" then, but that's how I felt.

Of course, Jackie had far worse things happen to him than I ever did, but there I was, in a place where no black man had ever been. I played one more game down in Boston and then went back to the Quebec Aces. But now I had tasted the big time; it's a taste that you never forget. I knew that I would be back.

CHAPTER ELEVEN
WAITING

The summer after my debut with the Boston Bruins, I got another letter from them. Again I was being invited back to training camp. Again I was thrilled. Again Stan Maxwell received a letter, too, and away we went.

It was good to be back in Boston. In one year I had come a long way. I had been to the Bruins training camp, I had been cut, then I had been called up by the big club. I had played two games for them, winning one in Montreal 3-0, and losing the other 6-2 in Boston. My parents came down to see me play in Boston, which made breaking the color barrier even sweeter, despite the fact we lost the game.

So at this training camp, I felt like a veteran. I knew the drills, and the team knew me. It was great to see the guys again, and I was confident that this time I would make the team. I trained and played hard, but when training camp ended, the Bruins said I needed to go back to Quebec — for seasoning.

Boston had made it to the Stanley Cup finals in 1958 and lost 4 games to 2 against — who else? — the Montreal Canadiens. The Bruins had also lost to the Canadiens in the finals the year before, 4 games to 1. Maybe Lynn Patrick figured that he had the lineup to win the Cup and didn't want to tinker with it. As I said earlier, the guys playing in the NHL knew that there were a lot of other guys playing in leagues beneath them, so everyone was trying their best.

Even so, I wanted to be in the NHL. I felt that I had shown my stuff to the Bruins, and now they should show their faith in me. Sitting around wanting it to happen wasn't going to make it happen, so I just said I'm going to work harder.

Little did I know how true that was going to be. In the same season that I made my debut with the Bruins, I also debuted for the Springfield Indians, and I sure wasn't glad about that. Playing in Springfield was like being sent to the worst place you could imagine — hell and the North Pole in winter all in one. This wasn't because the town of Springfield, in southern Massachusetts, was a bad place. It was because the owner and manager and coach and general know-it-all of the Springfield Indians was one Eddie Shore. And he was the most miserable guy in hockey.

I mentioned Eddie Shore earlier. He was a Stanley Cup champion with the Boston Bruins and one of the best defensemen who ever played the game. He was. He was also one of hockey's most colorful characters ever, and he deserves mention because they don't make them like Eddie anymore.

Eddie Shore became a hockey player because of teasing. Though he loved other sports, Eddie's older brother felt there was something un-Canadian about Eddie's apparent lack of interest in hockey. Shore was hurt by the teasing, so he pursued hockey like a bull chases a red flag. He'd practice outside when it was 40° below zero. Frost would form on his back and shoulders. His nose and cheeks and feet would freeze. He was determined to be a hockey player.

He succeeded and played in the minors in the early 1920s. As a member of the Melville Millionaires, in a 1924 championship match against the Winnipeg Monarchs, Shore's coach told him to stay out of the penalty box. Shore liked to fight, so this was hard for him, but he obeyed. Winnipeg took advantage of his gentlemanly play and knocked him out cold three times. Shore lost six teeth and broke both his nose and his jaw. But his team won the game.

Shore was the toughest piece of meat in the butcher's shop. In his hockey career, he had 14 broken noses, and he took 978 stitches. Despite this, Shore had no scars. He believed that wounds should be stitched cleanly and then seriously massaged to stop scar tissue from forming. At his first NHL training camp in 1926, the rookie Shore got in a fight with a veteran and knocked the guy out. Shore was hurt, too, his ear split down the middle and flapping in the breeze. A team doctor wanted to amputate, but Shore said, "Nope." He found another doctor who would sew the ear back together. He took nothing to kill the pain and watched the whole operation in a mirror — to direct the doctor's stitching, so there wouldn't be a scar.

By the time I caught up with him, he was the 56-year-old boss of the Springfield Indians. NHL coaches used to threaten to send problem players to Eddie Shore to make them learn how to behave. Shore was unbelievable. He called us all "Mister" and was very polite, but it didn't fool anyone.

Some of the things he did were crazy. He would act as a chiropractor (someone who manipulates your bones to relieve pain), even though he wasn't, and he would end up injuring the players he treated. He would make us practice in the dark to save electricity. He would make his goalies use skates so small they would lose toenails. Once, he even traded a player for a hockey net, then complained that the net was used.

He didn't think much of me. I don't know why. It wasn't race, it was just Eddie. In the first game, I warmed up, then I sat on the bench for the rest of the game. It was the same thing for the next four games. In the sixth game, at the 14-minute mark of the third period, one of our guys got hurt. Shore put me on the ice. I was cold, I hadn't played for five and two-thirds games. So I went out there. We started playing. I went to pick up the puck and tripped on a piece of debris on the ice. I went down. Shore yanked me out of the game, and the next morning, he told me that I was going back to Quebec.

I was happy to be getting out of there, but I was also angry. "What did you bring me down here for if you were just going to leave me on the bench?" I asked him.

His reply was classic Eddie Shore: "You can't skate right, you can't play with the puck, you can't backcheck right. I thought you were a better hockey player."

I didn't know whether to laugh or yell at him. So I asked, "How do you know what kind of hockey player I am? You haven't even let me play!" Then I walked out of there and got on the train back to Quebec. I vowed that I would do everything to avoid ever seeing Eddie Shore again.

And for the 1958-59 season I did. I played back in Quebec for the Aces, and the following year, I was sent to Kingston, to play for the Frontenacs. Kingston, approximately halfway between Toronto and Montreal, is often the butt of jokes. People say that Kingston has a military college, a federal prison, a mental hospital, and a university, and that it's sometimes difficult to tell one from the other.

Kingston was and is a first-class hockey town. I had a great season playing with Cal Gardner, who was also the coach. He had played for New York, Toronto, Chicago, and Boston. The fact that he was now in Kingston made me feel that it was okay that I was there, too. Besides, he was 34 and I was a decade younger. In fact, I had my best pro season so far in Kingston. I scored 21 goals and added 25 assists for a total of 46 points.

I also had my first serious girlfriend in Kingston. Her name was Lynn Campbell, and she was working in research at Queen's University. I used to see a lot of her, as she was a great hockey fan. She was also white. My mother and dad were of the old school, however, and they believed that you had to marry within your race. They weren't racists, they were just trying to protect me. "What would people say if they saw you with a white girl?" was how they thought.

As far as I was concerned, it wasn't anybody's business but mine and Lynn's. Still, there was truth in what my parents said. In some places in the United States, a white woman and a black man together ran the risk of being killed. Things were that bad.

I was at home after the season ended, and I told my mother that I was going up to Kingston to see Lynn. I asked mom if she would like to come, and she said yes. So we went, and we visited with Lynn, but I could see that my mother wasn't happy about the fact that Lynn and I weren't of the same race. My parents had given me so much, and it was important to me to keep them happy — even if it meant denying myself. So Lynn and I parted company.

I saw her again a couple of years ago in Fredericton. A film was made about my life, and she came to the first showing of it and to the party afterwards. It was good to see her again after 40 years. Life is like that. You have to say good-bye to people you don't always want to say good-bye to. But it's nice when you get to say hello again.

So I finished the 1959-60 season in Kingston. The NHL scouts had seen how well I played. The question was whether or not they would invite me to come back to the big league. I knew that my two games in 1958 weren't enough to convince them. I had worked hard, and I had improved. A 21-goal season is a very good one by any standards. And I did it all with only one eye.

I'm 19 years old when I push off from the boards as a Quebec Frontenac, with Walter Bradley. I played for the Frontenacs of the Quebec Junior Hockey League in the 1954-55 season, and it was there that my coach, Phil Watson, a former NHL star, first told me that I, too, had the skills and talent to make it as a pro.

My first taste of professional hockey came as a member of the Quebec Aces from 1956 to 1959. Under the guidance of "Punch" Imlach, I showed the NHL scouts that I could play in the big league.

I'm as proud as I can be in my Boston Bruins home uniform in 1961. I worked extremely hard over the years to get to this point, and nothing — including racism, and blindness in one eye — could stop me.

I'm driving to the net after shooting the puck past the Montreal Canadiens' Tom Johnson. It's a historic date: January 18, 1958, the night of my first NHL game — and the first time a black man ever played in the NHL.

Here I'm stickhandling the puck as a member or the Los Angeles Blades of the Western Hockey League. When I first heard that I had been traded to LA in 1961, I was surprised to learn that they had ice hockey in the land of palm trees and surfing.

This is me spraying ice chips as a San Diego Gull of the Western Hockey League. I had a great time in San Diego during my seven seasons with the team — and I had my best pro year there, too, scoring 79 points in 1968-69.

Here I am scoring a game-winning goal for the New Haven Nighthawks during the 1972-73 season when I was loaned to New Haven for 50 games. I had also started wearing a helmet as a result of receiving too many bumps on my head.

I love working with young people, and here I'm teaching some young Southern California hockey players during a coaching clinic. When I played for San Diego from 1967 to 1974, I conducted nearly 20 such clinics for kids from ages six to 17. It set me up nicely for my future job with the NHL.

It's Willie O'Ree Day at Boston's Fleet Center on January 31, 1998, and the Bruins gave me a jersey with my old number on it. I also got to meet Bruins captain Ray Bourque and one of the brightest young black stars, Anson Carter. What a thrill!

This is me now, as the Director of Youth Development for the NHL/USA Hockey Diversity Task Force. This isn't what I wear to work these days, though — it's my old San Diego Gulls gear. Behind me on the wall are mementos from my lifetime in hockey.

No one except Stan Maxwell and my family knew that I was blind in one eye. If the NHL ever found out, I was finished. They had a policy that prevented people with sight in only one eye from playing for them. They didn't want anyone to lose their other eye. And no insurance company would ever insure a player with one eye. I wasn't worried that my secret would get out. I just wanted to make sure that my great season in Kingston didn't remain a secret. Soon I would find out that the Bruins knew all about it.

CHAPTER TWELVE

THE BLACK BEAR

In the 1960-61 season, it finally happened. I got the call from the Bruins that I had been waiting for. They had seen what I had done in Kingston, so in December 1960, they asked me to come back to Boston — for good.

"Just bring your skates," they said. This meant that they were going to provide me with equipment and sticks. I was on the team! I took the train down to Boston and stayed with my cousin out in Roxbury (a suburb of Boston which is home mainly to black people). I would have to take the train into Boston Garden for the games.

Once again, the media didn't make a big deal of the fact that I was the first and only black man to play in the NHL. I didn't care so much for myself, but it would have been nice for other black kids to read about me. Imagine if you were the only black kid on a hockey team somewhere in North America and you read about the first black man in the NHL. It would make you play harder, so that you could be the second.

Not many black people went to games in those days, either. The Bruins were great about getting the team tickets when we needed them. If you wanted five or six seats for a game, it was no problem. So I increased the black attendance at Boston Garden all by myself. I'd get tickets and give them to my cousin and people in Roxbury. Of course my parents came to see me play, and so did my brother Richard. I was so proud when he saw me wearing the black and gold, with number 22 on the back. (In those days they didn't put your name on the back, so people knew you by your number.) All those dreams that I had told Richard about on Island Lake and on the ice rinks of Fredericton had come true!

I loved life in the NHL. I loved traveling to New York and Chicago and Detroit and Toronto and Montreal on the train. In those days, teams would play back-to-back games in each other's rinks, so we'd travel on the train together. Since there were only six teams, rivalries were intense. Imagine being on the same train with a guy you had dropped the gloves with just a couple of hours earlier. We kept to our separate railcars, but you would bump into the other teams on the way to the dining car. It could get tense, but mostly we had fun with the guys on the team. We'd play cards, tell stories, and generally kid around like teams do.

I also loved getting to play against some of the best guys in hockey. There was Gordie Howe in Detroit, who was so strong and so gifted. He could make plays happen out of nothing. But you didn't want to go into the corners with him. Though he was nicknamed "Mr. Hockey," he was also called "Mr. Elbows." If you went into a corner with Gordie, you'd be seeing stars when his elbow connected to your chin.

I also admired Terry Sawchuk, who played goal for the Red Wings. He was a moody guy, but he was some great goalie. Most nights the puck looked like a beachball to Sawchuk. He could stop everything. He'd dive and kick and bat the puck. He'd stop it with his head if he had to. And he didn't wear a mask either.

The first goalie to wear a mask was Jacques Plante, in 1959. Even though goalies were staring at pieces of frozen rubber rocketing at their heads, they didn't really start wearing masks until the late '60s. Sawchuk often got hurt, but he was a tough guy. And we had something in common.

When he was 18, a stick caught him in *his* right eye during a game. The doctor wanted to cut out Terry's eye but then changed his mind. He sewed up the eye, and Terry later regained his sight. He went on to win four Vezina Trophies as the NHL's best goalie. He also won four Stanley Cups and posted 103 shutouts in 971 regular-season games. No one will ever beat that.

Even though I was in the NHL and knew that the Bruins wanted to keep me, I played every game as if it was my last one. I knew if I worked hard, I would get what I now wanted more than anything: my first NHL goal.

On January 1, 1961, we were playing at home against Montreal. It was a huge game. People were still celebrating New Year, and the Montreal Canadiens were always a hot ticket. It was like being at two parties at once.

The Canadiens were as glamorous as ever in their red, white, and blue jerseys. They had won the Stanley Cup the year before (their fifth in a row), and they still had some of the best players to ever play the game. Bernie "Boom-Boom" Geoffrion was putting pucks in the net left and right, and close behind him was Jean Beliveau. My hero, Rocket Richard, had retired, but the Canadiens had a deep lineup. They also had a strong farm-team system, and it looked as if they would be unbeatable again that season.

It was a tough game, with both sides fighting hard. Halfway through the third period, we had a 2-1 lead. Both teams had a man in the penalty box, so there was a lot of ice. I took a pass from Leo Boivin and turned on the speed. I have always been blessed with quick acceleration. I would just have to take a couple of steps, and I'd be gone. With the open ice, I had a lot of room with which to work.

I sped by Montreal defenseman Jean-Guy Talbot just inside the Canadiens blue line. Then Tom Johnson came

The Black Bear

after me, but he broke his stick trying to stop me. Suddenly, I was all alone in front of goalie Charlie Hodge.

I had played against Charlie before. He had been the backstopper for the Montreal Royals when I played for the Quebec Aces. Charlie was a little guy, maybe 5 feet 6 inches (168 cm) tall and 150 pounds (68 kg). Players are always saying that they're bigger than they are in game programs, so Charlie could have been smaller than that. Because he was small, I always used to shoot high on him, and I had scored on him in Quebec doing just that.

Before that game against the Canadiens, my teammate Bronco Horvath saw me shooting in the practice session. Bronco played center, and the year before he had come second in the scoring race, with 80 points in a 70-game season. Bronco had potted 39 goals and added 41 assists. He was only one point behind Bobby Hull of Chicago, who notched one more assist. And Bronco had played 68 games— two less than Hull! So he knew how to put the puck in the net.

When he saw me practicing, he said, "O'Ree, you're shooting too high. You have to keep your shots low." He explained that up high, the goalie has his pads, his glove, his stick, his blocker, and his body. But down low, he just has his stick on the ice. I knew this, but I figured I could put the puck past Hodge if I shot high.

Even so, when I found myself in alone on Charlie Hodge, Bronco's words came into my brain. "Shoot low, shoot low!" I heard. So I let the puck rip along the ice, and bang! The red light was on, and thousands of people were cheering for me. It was my first NHL goal, and I was overjoyed. I dove into the net and fished the puck out, then skated it over to the bench. I gave it to our coach, Milt Schmidt, and I told him to look after it for me. He smiled and promised that he would. I still have that puck at home.

For two minutes afterwards, people in the Boston Garden just stood and cheered — for me! It was amazing. Look at your watch and time two minutes. It's a long time. I didn't know where to look after a while. I knew the fans in Boston were on my side, but I didn't realize how much.

Back home in Fredericton, my parents heard the news. I had scored my first goal, and the 14,000 fans at the Boston Garden showed what they thought of me. Not only was it my first goal, it turned out to be the winning goal because Henri Richard scored to make it 3-2. But my goal stood. My parents were delighted about everything. It looked like their fears that I would be rejected in the white world of big-league pro hockey were gone. I was a real NHLer now.

CHAPTER THIRTEEN

THE BLACK BEAR FIGHTS BACK

In 1961, the civil rights movement was just beginning. This was a social-protest action aimed at helping American blacks become more equal to white people in society. I'm sorry to say that the civil rights movement was not part of the pro hockey world.

The media didn't make a big deal about me being the first black man to play in the NHL, but some of the other players did. And not in a good way, either. Now don't get me wrong. I've never had a problem with any of my teammates on the 11 pro teams for which I've played. The guys wearing the same jersey as me were great. They were supportive, and considerate, and rooting for me. The problem was with the players on the other teams.

I never had any trouble with the Montreal Canadiens or the Toronto Maple Leafs. Canada likes to think of itself as a more tolerant society than the United States, and maybe it is, though I have had my problems at home. The real reason, I think, that I was left alone when Boston played in Canada was because players and fans knew me from my junior and minor pro days. I was a familiar face.

In the United States, I was a black face. I used to hear ugly name-calling in New York, Detroit, and Chicago. Guys would take runs at me to knock me into the boards, and they would cross-check me. There wasn't a game back then when there wasn't an ugly racial remark directed at me.

Once I went up to the referee and said, "This guy just called me a nasty name." And he said, "What do you want me to do about it?" Today, the NHL takes racial incidents very seriously. Players who are guilty of insulting another player because of his race are punished with heavy fines and are embarrassed in the media. Back then, though, that didn't exist. I knew I was going to have to look after myself. I never had any problems with the referees, but it was in Chicago on the ice that I had my worst experience with another player.

It was my first trip to Chicago Stadium, and I was looking forward to playing the Black Hawks and learning something from their big star, Bobby Hull, who was called "The Golden Jet" (he's the father of Brett Hull of the Dallas Stars). Bobby Hull was amazing. With forearms like Popeye, he was strong as a bull and fast, too. But Bobby Hull's big gun was his shot. It was so hard it scared goalies, and it made other guys' shots look weak.

Bobby played left wing like me, but he liked to shoot from the slot. When he did, more often than not the red light would flash and Bobby Hull would notch another goal. He had won the Art Ross Trophy as the NHL's scoring champion the season before and would win it twice more before he was finished. In fact, four of the first six 50-goal seasons in the NHL belong to Bobby Hull. With his blond hair flowing as he made an unbelievable end-to-end rush, he was something to watch.

Chicago also had future Hall-of-Famers Glenn Hall in goal and Stan Mikita at center. Hall had reflexes so fast that you thought he must be a magician. Shooters figured they had him beat, and suddenly his glove hand would whip out and he'd snatch the puck in midair. He was so nervous before games that he used to throw up, but once he was on the ice, he made shooters nervous with his talent.

The Black Bear Fights Back

Stan Mikita had talent in bucket loads. He won the NHL scoring title four times in five years. He won the Hart Trophy as the NHL's Most Valuable Player twice. He also was one tough customer, but that's because of his tough childhood. His parents had shipped him out of his native Czechoslovakia in 1948, when Stan was just eight years old. They did this because they didn't want him to grow up behind the "Iron Curtain" of the Soviet Union's Communist dictatorship. So Stan came to live with his aunt and uncle in Canada. He didn't speak English, and he looked different, so the other kids gave him a hard time. Stan fought back and kept on fighting back right into the NHL. I knew how he felt. Stan eventually changed his style and won the Lady Byng Trophy twice for gentlemanly play.

So there I was in the old Chicago Stadium with all these stars, looking forward to a great game. They played the national anthem on that big Wurlitzer organ, and the fans went wild. That old organ did make the hairs stand up on your neck. I was pumped! This was exciting! But it didn't last long.

In fact, the game was less than two minutes old when trouble hit. It was just the second shift of the first period when Chicago right-winger Eric Nesterenko skated up to me and called me the "n-word." Nesterenko was big: 6 foot 2 (188 cm) and about 200 pounds (91 kg). He was rough, too, and his nickname was "Elbows."

So he called me that nasty name, and before I had time to respond, he took his stick and butt-ended me in the mouth. Butt-ending is one of the dirtiest things you can do in hockey. If you've never seen a butt-end (and I hope you haven't and if you have, then I hope you never use it), then this is what happens. A guy will lower his hand on the top part of his stick, to expose wood. Then he'll jam that top part of the stick into another guy. The butt-end is nothing more than an attempt to injure another player.

Eric Nesterenko's butt-end sure injured me. He knocked my two front teeth out, he split my lip, and he broke my nose. Then he stood there, smiling, and said the n-word again. I knew that he had butt-ended me on purpose, and then he tried to high stick me! I ducked under it and smacked him on the head with my stick. I cut him pretty good, and it took 14 or 15 stitches to close him up.

The blood was flowing from my mouth and from his head, but he wasn't ready to quit. He was mad that the black man had fought back, so he went after me. He grabbed me, and we went up against the glass. He was bigger than I was, so he had a longer arm reach. I grabbed him to make sure that he couldn't punch me.

Meanwhile, both benches had cleared and everyone was fighting. The fans were hollering something fierce at me because some of them figured all of this was my fault — for fighting back. Finally the linesmen broke it up, and Nesterenko and I each got five-minute penalties for drawing blood.

They took me to the Boston dressing room to fix me up. They plugged up my broken nose and washed off the blood. I wanted to go back out and play, but the trainer said it was too dangerous. The Chicago officials had said there would be "injuries" if I went back in. What did this mean?

Well, I guess that Chicago felt that they couldn't control their own fans or players. So guess what happened? They locked me in the Boston dressing room for the rest of the game — for my own protection. There wasn't any TV in there like there is today, so for nearly the whole game, I sat alone wondering what was happening out on the ice. So

The Black Bear Fights Back

much for seeing Bobby Hull and Stan Mikita and Glenn Hall. I was a prisoner in Chicago Stadium.

After the game, things were still tense. The Chicago officials told us that we'd need a police escort to get out of the rink safely. The police marched us to our bus, but there wasn't any trouble. We got on the bus and out of Chicago. When I spoke to my parents they had read all about my fight, but the newspapers didn't tell the whole story. It just said that "Willie O'Ree and Eric Nesterenko had a bloody stick-duel in Chicago." I didn't tell my parents what really happened. And I never did. For the rest of their lives, they never knew the truth. It would have hurt them too much.

I had to go back to Chicago again later that season. I figured there would be big trouble this time. I was sure that Eric Nesterenko wanted to pay *me* back for cutting his head open, but nothing happened. He took a couple of physical shots at me in later games, but nothing was even close to that butt-end, and he didn't call me any names. Maybe he learned his lesson, maybe he didn't.

Almost by magic, I had a chance to find out 30 years later. In 1991, I received a call from the NHL inviting me to the All-Star Game in Chicago. I was surprised because I hadn't heard from the NHL in a long time. Still, I was pleased at the invitation, so I went. The NHL put me up in the luxurious Drake Hotel and paid all my expenses. It was a wonderful time. Chicago is a really great city, with wonderful architecture, restaurants, art galleries, and people.

So I went to my first All-Star function, and who was there but Bobby Hull and Stan Mikita. The guys I had missed seeing play in my first game in Chicago, because I was locked in the dressing room, were now in the same room as me. It was a great feeling.

I walked up to the bar to get myself a glass of beer. Guess who was standing next to me? Eric Nesterenko. I turned to look at him, and he said, "Hi, Willie, how's it going?" I said, "Not too bad." I turned away, and he didn't say anything more. I figured that his violent attack on me was something that happened a long time ago. What good would it do to bring it up now? It would have been nice to hear him say, "I'm sorry." But I don't think I ever will.

CHAPTER FOURTEEN
A BEAR NO MORE

I was a Boston Bruin for 43 games during that 1960-61 season. In those days, seasons weren't as long as they are now because there weren't as many teams. We only played 70 games, so I was up with the big club for more than half the season. Now that I had a taste of life in the NHL (even if it was sometimes a bad taste), I wanted more.

Things looked good for me, even if they didn't look so good for the Bruins. I scored four goals and added 10 assists, and I made $9,000 for my work. The Bruins were the lowest-scoring team in the NHL, and out of our 70 games that season, we only won 15. We lost 42, we tied 13, and we finished in last place with 43 points — 11 points behind New York, who were second last. It was the beginning of a rough patch for the Bruins. The team would finish in last place for the next four seasons, then in second last, and then in last again until they put this talented kid named Bobby Orr on defense.

But I didn't know any of this back in the summer of 1961. All I knew was that I had a future with the Bruins. Before I left for home after our last game, I was invited into the office of coach Milt Schmidt and manager Lynn Patrick. They were laughing and friendly and made me relax. "We're very impressed with your play this season," they told me. Even better, they promised me a future. "Look forward to being back with the Bruins next season," they said. "Now go home and have a great summer!"

I was so happy! I had passed the test, and now my life in the NHL looked secure. I was going to be a Boston Bruin next season, and the season after that, and with luck, for the rest of my NHL career. I hustled home to Fredericton and told everyone what the Bruins had said. My mom and dad were thrilled, my friends were pleased, and my brother Richard was even prouder of me. I felt like a star.

I was at home for about six weeks when a long-distance call came for me. My mom answered the phone and said, "Willie, it's a sportswriter from the *Telegraph-Journal*." The *Telegraph-Journal* was the newspaper in the city of St. John, New Brunswick. As I went to take the phone, I thought that maybe the writer wanted to do a feature piece on me. I could see the headline: "New Brunswick Kid Makes Good in the NHL." No one had written such a story yet, and I figured that after my 43 games in the NHL, it wouldn't be a risk to write one now.

I picked up the phone and said hello. The sportswriter told me his name, then asked, "Willie, what do you think of the trade?" My heart skipped a beat. Why would a sportswriter be asking me about a trade? "You have me at a disadvantage," I said. "I don't know what trade you mean."

The sportswriter explained that news had just come out, and it involved me. "You've been traded to the Montreal Canadiens for Cliff Pennington and Terry Gray," said the sportswriter. "How do you feel about playing for the Montreal Canadiens?"

What? I had been traded to Montreal? But the Bruins said that I would be back playing in Boston next year! They told me to go home and enjoy myself! No one from the Bruins had called me to tell me that I had been traded. And here was a writer on the other end of the phone line asking how I felt.

Shocked and speechless is how I felt, but speechless doesn't translate too well into a newspaper article. "Well," I

A Bear No More

began, thinking about the reality of this news, "if I have been traded, then I won't be playing for *the* Montreal Canadiens. I'll probably be playing for one of their farm teams." Montreal had won five straight Stanley Cups from 1955-56 to 1959-60. They finished first with 92 points in the season we had just finished — nearly 50 points better than the 43 we got in Boston! Montreal had brilliant players like Jean Beliveau, Henri Richard, Dickie Moore, Bernie "Boom-Boom" Geoffrion, and a bunch more coming up. I didn't figure that they needed me to complete their lineup.

On the other hand, I had proven myself in the NHL. I was 25 years old, so I was still young enough to get another shot — if my suspicions were right. Sure enough, I received a nice letter from Montreal's farm team, the Hull-Ottawa Canadiens. It was written by Sam Pollock, the team manager, who said that Montreal had acquired my contract from Boston, but they wanted me to report to Hull-Ottawa. I mean, the wind was right out of my sails. I had gone from the NHL to the minor leagues just like that.

I'm sure that my parents and brother were as disappointed as I was, but they tried to make me feel better. I had taken a lot of knocks before, but this one was hard because I had been set up to believe the opposite. As I prepared to go to Hull-Ottawa, the words of Lynn Patrick and Milt Schmidt kept running through my head. "Look forward to being back with the Bruins next season," they had said. "Now go home and have a great summer!" It's hard to have a great summer when the future that you had hoped for, and the one that you had been promised, disappears just like that.

I waited and waited for the Bruins to call me up to explain why they did what they did, but no call ever came. I didn't have a high-powered agent who could call the Bruins and demand an answer. I didn't have one because nobody had one. Hockey agents didn't exist yet. So to this day, I don't know why the Bruins let me go. Both the guys they traded me for went on to play over 100 games each in the NHL, so at least I know the Bruins weren't trading me to the minor leagues on purpose.

But it wasn't going to do me any good to dwell on what had been. I resolved to go to the Canadiens' farm team and do what I always did. I'd work hard, and that work would be rewarded with a shot at pulling on the red, white, and blue jersey of the Montreal Canadiens. Once they had seen how badly I wanted to be the best player I could be, I knew that they would give me a tryout. After all, they wouldn't have traded for me if they hadn't seen what I could do in the NHL. And I was going to try my best to make them see what I could do in the NHL once again.

CHAPTER FIFTEEN

GOING SOUTH

Going to play for the Canadiens — the *Hull-Ottawa* Canadiens — wasn't a complete unknown because I had played in Hull-Ottawa before. In fact, I had played quite well for them at the beginning of the 1960-61 season. I potted 10 goals and added nine assists in 16 games. That's better than a point a game. I had figured that I was in for a pretty good year that season in Hull-Ottawa — until I got the phone call to play for the Boston Bruins. Now here I was back in Hull-Ottawa after being told by those same Bruins that I would be playing for them *this* season. You could say that life has its little jokes, though I wasn't laughing too hard at this one.

The Hull-Ottawa Canadiens practiced and played in Hull. The city is located in the province of Quebec, across the river from Canada's capital, Ottawa. The season before, when I was playing in Boston, the Hull-Ottawa Canadiens were burning up the Eastern Professional Hockey League. They finished in first place, with 91 points, and they won the league championship. It's always nice to be playing for a winner, and a large part of that was due to the brains behind the operation, Sam Pollock, the general manager.

Sam Pollock was 36 years old when I went to play for him that second time. Before he guided Hull-Ottawa to their championship, he had led the Junior Canadiens to two Memorial Cups — the Stanley Cup of junior hockey. Pollock had been with the Montreal Canadiens organization since he was 22 and would stay with them until he was 53, winning nine Stanley Cups as the team's general manager.

There was, however, a moment when he nearly got stopped before he got started in the Montreal organization.

"Disorganization" would be a good word to describe what was going on in Montreal at the end of the 1940s. While hockey was a religion in Montreal, there was no worship for the city's junior teams. They played fewer games than other junior teams. They often played late at night in the Montreal Forum, when fans — and players — were nodding off to sleep.

Then Montreal hired a brilliant hockey guy named Frank Selke, who had quit Toronto because he couldn't stand being bullied by Conn Smythe. Selke spent hundreds of thousands of dollars to build up the Canadiens' farm system. Sam Pollock, 22 years old, was then director of the Midget Canadiens — the younger kids who played in the Canadiens' system. The coach of the Junior Canadiens was leaving, so he told Frank Selke that Pollock should get his job.

There was a problem. Another guy who was the "honorary president" of the Junior Canadiens wanted the job to go to a friend of his. This friend was a local amateur hockey star, whose real job was in banking. Selke's response was simple: one man had chosen hockey, he said, and the other banking. So he hired Sam Pollock.

Pollock was built like a bulldog, and he had a mind to match. He would pursue his goals with fierce determination, and he was great at motivating everyone else around him. He was also smart and knew the value of not just his own players but also of everyone playing in every other league. Clearly, Sam Pollock was going places.

When I laced up my skates for the Hull-Ottawa Canadiens for the start of the 1961-62 season, I was looking forward to going places, too. And so I did, but not quite the way I imagined.

Going South

The season was only 12 games old when I showed up at the rink for a practice. In the dressing room was our trainer and one other player. It was about 8:15 in the morning, and we had our workout scheduled for 10. As soon as the trainer saw me, he said, "Willie, Sammy wants to see you." I told him that I'd see Pollock after the practice, but the trainer was definite. "No, he wants to see you right now. He's up in his office."

I didn't know what to think. When a general manager wants to see a player urgently, it could mean anything. I went up to Pollock's office, and he was sitting at his desk, with papers scattered all over the place. I asked him if he wanted to see me, and he said, "Yes, yes, come in."

I stood in front of his desk for a full 30 seconds, and Sam sat there with his head down. He didn't look at me once. I began to fear that something bad had happened to my parents, or to one of my brothers or sisters. Finally, he looked up and said, "Oh, yes, Willie, I'm glad that you're here."

He stood up and walked around to the front of his desk. He put his arm around my shoulders, and I noticed that he had this envelope in his hand. "Willie," he said, "from time to time the Montreal organization has to make changes in their player personnel" ("player personnel" is just a fancy way of saying "players"). He smiled at me in a kind of fatherly fashion, even though he was only 10 years older than me. "We've been impressed with your play, but we've traded you to..." To where? Back to the Boston Bruins I hoped. Back to anywhere in the NHL.

"We've traded you to the Los Angeles Blades in the Western Hockey League," he said. Wait a second, I thought, they don't even have a hockey team in Los Angeles! That's the land of football and baseball and palm trees. Pollock then handed me the envelope. Inside it was an airplane ticket.

"Your flight to Los Angeles leaves at 12:50," he said. "Today." It was now 8:30. I had just over four hours to pack up my gear, and my apartment, and my life, and catch that plane out west.

I went back to the dressing room and told the trainer I'd been traded to LA. He was pleased for me. "You'll be having fun out there with all those movie stars," he said. I wasn't convinced. I picked up my two pairs of skates and a couple dozen hockey sticks. Some of them were so new that I hadn't even taken them out of their cellophane wrapping.

I went back to my apartment and got my things together. I was single, and the apartment had been rented to me fully furnished, so I just had to pack my clothes and personal items. Then I went to the bank, took out some money, and headed off to the airport.

I had never been to the west coast, and I certainly had never imagined playing there. I had figured the Canadiens would give me a shot at the NHL after they saw me play in Hull-Ottawa. Now I was going to have to work my way up to the big leagues from as far away from the action as I could be. The closest NHL team to California was in Chicago. And that was nearly a couple of thousand miles away. I got on that plane to LA wondering if I would ever be back. Maybe I was finished with hockey. I was about to find out.

CHAPTER SIXTEEN

CALIFORNIA DREAMING

When I stepped out of the airplane in Los Angeles on November 12, 1961, the temperature was about 75° Fahrenheit (24° Celsius). When I had left Hull-Ottawa, it was freezing. I had been dressed for winter, and now here I was in what seemed like summer. I took off my heavy topcoat and walked down the steps of the plane. (In those days, you walked from the plane to the terminal across the tarmac.) I inhaled the warm evening air and looked around. The moon lit up the green palm trees. I couldn't believe that they had hockey here in what seemed like the tropics, but I was sure hoping that they did.

I caught a taxi to the Coliseum Hotel, and I signed in. As I was preparing to go up to my room, I noticed this guy reading a newspaper. I knew I had seen him before, but I knew he wasn't a movie star. He shifted the paper and turned his head, and suddenly I realized who it was: Jean-Marc Picard. I had played hockey against him in junior!

"Jean-Marc!" I called out.

"Hey, Willie," he said. "Have you been traded, too?"

We had both been dealt to the Los Angeles Blades, and we had a laugh at the coincidence. Instead of going to my room, I told the bell captain to take my gear up. I didn't even bother checking out the room to see if it was suitable. I was so happy to see a familiar face that I accepted Jean-Marc's invitation to go out and see the sights of LA.

Well, see the sights we did. My previous home of Hull, Quebec, was famous for its nightlife, but LA made it look like a sleepy village. The town was hopping, and Jean-Marc and I wound up at the Whiskey A Go-Go in Hollywood. It's a famous nightclub, and we had a great time listening to Sam & Dave, a famous singing group. We told stories and had a beer or two.

We had so much fun catching up, that I didn't get back to my hotel room until 2 AM. With the time zone difference, it was 5 AM in Hull-Ottawa. I had been awake for nearly 24 hours, I had crossed the continent, and I had been a member of two different hockey teams. It had been quite a day.

The next morning, Jean-Marc and I had a meeting at the Sports Arena, which is where the Blades played. We were welcomed onto the team by the coach and given our Blades uniforms and gear. Then we had a practice, and that night we were playing the Calgary Stampeders (the hockey, not the football, team).

It's an amazing feeling to have your whole world turned upside down like that. Imagine waking up one morning and being told that you were going to a new school in a new city. You might not even have a chance to say good-bye to your friends. Then you have to show up at the new school and fit right in. You miss your old school, and you miss your friends, but you can't go back. That's what being traded is like.

In hockey, you have new teammates and you're playing in a new rink, but at least the game is the same. California was agreeing with me because I got a couple of goals in that first game. The fans cheered me on as if I had always been there, and the papers said something like, "The addition of Willie O'Ree is a good one." There's nothing like scoring a couple of goals and getting a win to make you feel at home.

In my second season, my old friend Stan Maxwell came to play in LA. There we were, the only two black guys in the

California Dreaming

WHL. The league was a good one, too. A very good league. The more we played, the more I loved it. For one thing, we would get 8,000 people out for a game. In Hull-Ottawa, we would average only 2,000. The fans were great. And they sure knew their hockey. That wasn't surprising, really.

Firstly, Los Angeles had been home to minor pro teams since the 1920s. There had been the Los Angeles Palais-de-Glace (which is French for "Ice Palace") in 1925-26. There had been company teams like Richfield Oil and the Globe Ice Cream. There had been the Millionaires (whose name would be appropriate to describe players' salaries today). There were the Angels in 1931-32, and from 1948 to 1950, the city boasted the Los Angeles Monarchs, who were a farm team for the NHL's Toronto Maple Leafs.

Secondly, Los Angeles has a huge Canadian population. A lot of Canadians moved south to work in the film and television industry, and a lot moved south for the weather. Not all of our fans were Canadians, but there were enough of them.

I also liked playing in LA because I fell in love there. Well, not exactly there, but on the road, in Portland. Her name was Bernadine Plummer, and she was going to university. She was also a Portland Buckaroos fan. She had an aunt living in California, so moving down there wasn't too much of a shock for her. We were married in 1962, back home in Fredericton. My parents were thrilled, partly because Berna Deanne was black. As I said before, because this was important to them, it was important to me.

We set up house in Los Angeles, and before I knew it, I was a father. Our son, Kevin, was born in 1963, and then Darren in 1965. Suddenly, I was family man with family responsibilities. It's not the easiest role when you're a hockey player since you're on the road so much of the year.

The Blades traveled quite far compared to the eastern teams, who were mostly all packed together in one small region. At first we'd go all the way up the west coast and into the Canadian prairies: San Francisco, Portland, Spokane, Seattle, Vancouver, Calgary, and Edmonton. Then Calgary and Edmonton folded, and Denver and Victoria came into the league.

I liked seeing these new places, and I was knocked out by the beauty of the west. Everywhere you looked there was some beautiful place that you could put on a postcard. Everywhere but Portland, Oregon, that is. Now I know that Portland is one of the prettiest cities in the United States, but I didn't like playing there. The Portland Buckaroos had a rink that was smaller than NHL regulation, and they used it to their advantage.

For example, the Portland guys would know exactly how long it took the puck to get around the boards. Those of us used to the bigger rink would think it would take a second or two longer to get the puck, so we'd be a step late. Then bam! The Portland guys would run us into the boards hard. It wasn't fun to play in Portland.

There was another reason that I didn't like the place. One of the Portland Buckaroos used to give me an awful time. He'd always hit me from behind or spear me. He would call me ugly racial names (including the n-word), but he would never drop his gloves and fight me like a man. I had terrible stick fights with that guy because he was such a coward. It's amusing to me that this guy's son is a respected NHL star today, who has won a few Stanley Cups. This is one instance where you can't say "like father, like son".

In my first season with Los Angeles, I scored 28 goals and added 26 assists. In my next season, I scored 25, and helped on 26 others. These numbers were some of my best

California Dreaming

ever, but things were going to get even better. Alf Pike, who had played forward for the New York Rangers in the 1940s (and won a Stanley Cup with them), came to coach the Blades.

Alf had been nicknamed "The Embalmer" (they're the guys who put special fluids in dead people to preserve the body for burial), but he sure gave life to my career. His solution to making me score even more goals was brilliant. Alf knew that I couldn't see out of my right eye, so he put me on right wing. Brilliant! Now I didn't have to worry about guys hitting me on my blind side because my blind side was closest to the boards.

When Alf made the switch in the 1964-65 season, I scored 38 goals and added 21 assists. That was my highest goal total since I had been a pro hockey player. I won the WHL scoring title — the first time I had ever done so as a pro. I was thrilled, and so were the fans. It was just too bad that we didn't make the playoffs because those Los Angeles fans sure deserved it.

So there I was having a great time in California. In a few short years, I had been married, started a family, and become a star on the ice rink in Los Angeles. My life had sure changed, and I was happy. Then I heard something else that had the power to make me even happier. The NHL had decided to give Los Angeles an NHL franchise in 1967. I had played in the NHL and I was the leading scorer on the LA Blades. It looked like the Montreal Canadiens had done me a huge favor in sending me west. Once I thought that I had gone as far away from the NHL as a man could get, but now the NHL was coming right to my own backyard. I couldn't wait.

CHAPTER SEVENTEEN

HOCKEY AND SALSA

In the summer of 1967, the United States was going through a crisis, and I was living in the middle of it. There was the war in Vietnam, and there was a war at home — a war between the races. Two summers before, black people had rioted in a section of Los Angeles called Watts. They were angry about their treatment by white society for the past 200 years. Anger is one thing, but violence is another, and Watts was violent. Hundreds of buildings were burned, 34 people were killed, 1,000 injured, and 4,000 more arrested.

Buildings were burning again in 1967, when black people rioted in Detroit and other eastern cities. It was so severe that the National Guard was called in to stop it. For me, a black Canadian living in the United States, it was a troubled time. I wasn't political, but my very color put me on one side of the battle. All my life I had battled what people thought of my color as I tried to play hockey. I had made it to the NHL, and my color was no longer an issue for me. But everywhere I turned, color *was* the dominant issue of the day. More than ever, I was a "black" hockey player.

As far as I was concerned, I was going to be an NHL hockey player again. There was big excitement about the Kings coming to LA, and I was excited, too. Oddly enough, it was my old Hull-Ottawa general manager, Sam Pollock, who had a hand in the NHL coming to Southern California. Sam had moved up to the big Canadiens in 1964, and his talents were soon seen by everyone. He was asked by the league to head up a committee, looking at putting a few new teams into the mix.

TV was pumping a lot of money into sports in the United States, and hockey wanted a piece of the action. They needed more teams in big American cities to make the league attractive to television, so Pollock and his committee recommended that the NHL expand in 1967. The Original Six teams would now take to the ice against a whole new division. There would be the North Stars in Minnesota, the Penguins in Pittsburgh, the Flyers in Philadelphia, the Blues in St. Louis, the Seals in Oakland, and the Kings in Los Angeles.

So the NHL was coming to town, and I wanted another piece of it. I waited for a phone call or a letter inviting me to show my stuff at the Kings' training camp, but nothing happened. What could be the reason? I had proven my scoring touch in the WHL, and I had played in the NHL before. Surely it wasn't my color again, not in the times we were living in?

Finally, the phone rang. On the other end was Max McNab, the general manager of the San Diego Gulls. The Gulls had come into the Western Hockey League in the 1966-67 season, and they hadn't done very well. They needed help.

Max had played a couple of seasons for the Detroit Red Wings in the late 1940s. He was a tall, strong center, but his NHL career had been cut short because of back surgery. Now he was asking me what I was going to do about *my* career. Max asked, "Willie, are you planning on playing hockey this year?" I was 32 years old, and to tell you the truth, I didn't know. Max said he'd help me make a decision. He wanted me to play for him.

I wasn't sure about anything. My marriage had broken up the year before, and Berna Deanne was gone. My sons had gone with her, to live in Texas. Both Kevin and Darren, even though they were still little guys, had shown an interest in hockey. I was looking forward to teaching them the game I loved. Hockey wasn't big yet in Texas, which seemed very far away from both Los Angeles and San Diego. I still managed to see them a bit, and they played hockey until they were 15 or 16. I told them, "Don't think that because your name is O'Ree that it's going to be easy." After all, it wasn't easy for me. And it sure wasn't easy having them live so far away.

On the other hand, I was "single" again. I was free to pick up and move just like I had done when I got traded to Los Angeles six years earlier. And hockey had been my life for 16 years. Why stop now?

I had put in six good seasons with Los Angeles. Maybe it was time for a change. So I drove down to San Diego. It's about a three-hour trip from LA, almost as far as the Mexican border. I used to think it strange to be playing hockey in Los Angeles, but playing in Mexico's backyard? Could hockey exist there?

I met with Max, and he was great. We went back and forth on my contract, and I got a price that I figured was pretty good. I liked San Diego, too. It is a much smaller city than Los Angeles and, if you can believe it, has an even better climate. San Diego was (and still is) a military town, with both the US Navy and the Marines having bases nearby. It also has a ton of history. When the Spanish settled California in the 18th century, San Diego was the first place where they set up camp. There is a real Spanish feel to the architecture and a Mexican feel to the city life. This is not surprising, since Mexico is about a 15-minute drive south.

It was a long way from Fredericton, but I figured, "Why not? I'm still young, and maybe if I have another great season or two, one of the NHL expansion teams will pick me up." So I signed with the Gulls. My old center iceman from LA, Warren Hynes, came down to San Diego, too, and we picked up where we left off.

I was still playing right wing and having a great time. In my first three seasons with the Gulls, I scored 83 goals and helped on 96 others. I won the scoring title again in 1968-69 with another 38-goal season and 41 assists. I was as good as I had ever been. And the NHL went on without me.

The world was still changing, fast. Black people were gaining rights, and amazing things were happening in science and technology, like heart transplants and people going to the moon. And as far as color went, that was no longer an issue. What was the issue was my old injury.

There was even more NHL expansion, with teams in Vancouver and Buffalo, but I knew that I wouldn't make it back in. The NHL had found out about my blind right eye. They still had that rule that stopped anyone who was blind in one eye from playing. So my career was going to be in the WHL. That was fine with me. I made guest appearances at sports dinners and on radio shows in San Diego. I was paid well for what I was doing, and I loved hockey more than ever. And I was a star because of me, not because of my color.

CHAPTER EIGHTEEN
HANGING UP MY SKATES

I played for San Diego until 1974. I was nearly 40 years old, and I had played hockey for a long time. I had seen and done a lot. Every hockey player dreads the day that you know is coming. It's the day when you have to hang up your skates. It's the day that you say good-bye to the game that has been your life.

A few things helped me make the decision that the time was right. One of them was love. I had been divorced for a few years, and I hadn't really been serious about any woman. Little did I know but that was about to change — and again, because I was a hockey player! When I was on the road with the Gulls in Victoria, I met this guy named Amrit who wanted to interview me. He was a Indo-Canadian, going to the University of Victoria, and he was doing a university paper on professional athletes.

I agreed to the interview, and we had a good discussion. As you know, I have lots of stories to tell. When we were finished, the man invited me to have dinner with him, and his sister. I accepted.

Her name was Deljeet, and she was a hockey fan! Well, she had three brothers who were hockey nuts, so I guess she couldn't escape it. We got talking and found that we had a lot in common. So I fell in love with the sister of the guy who wanted to interview me because I was a hockey player. Her parents were against our relationship because it would mean that she was marrying outside of *her* race. I had been all through that earlier, but we got married anyway, in San Diego, on November 6, 1969.

Deljeet moved to San Diego, and we set up house. I still played for the Gulls, but I was loaned to the New Haven Nighthawks for part of the 1972-73 season. Loaning was fairly common practice, so we went off to Connecticut.

Playing in the American Hockey League was an experience. And that's because race once again became an issue. Sure, I had been called nasty names in the WHL, and fans booed me in some places (maybe because I was black, maybe because I was one of the star players). But on the whole, it wasn't too bad. Then I went back to the east coast, and we had to play games in the South. Trouble.

When we would play in Tidewater, Virginia, people would yell at me, "Why aren't you out pickin' cotton?" (Picking cotton is what the slaves had to do.) They'd shout out the n-word, too, but the worst thing they did you'll never believe. They threw a live black cat out onto the ice while I was playing! I couldn't believe it either. The poor cat didn't know what had hit it. I skated out, picked it up, and gave it to the trainer. The fans were shouting and name-calling while I did it. That cat and I were both happy to get out of there.

I had another bad experience in Baltimore, Maryland, in 1973. We had won our game against the Baltimore Clippers, and a bunch of us went out for dinner. A couple of the guys were already in the restaurant when the rest of us arrived. There was this guy standing at the door who saw me and wouldn't let me in. "No blacks allowed," he said. I couldn't believe that either. It was 1973! The civil rights movement had stopped that kind of stuff. Or so I thought. But he wouldn't let me in, so one of the players that I was with went in and got the other guys out, and we left. I thought, for a minute, that I was back in Georgia in 1956.

I even had a problem renting a place to live in Connecticut. I called the rental agent, told her my name, and said I was playing for the New Haven hockey club. I wanted to rent her cottage on the lake. Boy, it was pretty. It reminded me of my trips to Island Lake up in New Brunswick.

The rental agent said that she would need me to pay a deposit. I said no problem, and we arranged to meet at the cottage that afternoon. I got there early, and I saw her car pull up. She got out and started to walk toward me. I got out of my car, and when she saw me, she slowed down. I knew exactly what was going to happen. She gave me this fake smile and said, "Oh, Mr. O'Ree, I tried to call you earlier. The cottage has been rented." She was lying through her teeth. At that point in my life, I could tell in a heartbeat when someone was a racist. And she was.

So I was happy to get back to San Diego. I played for the Gulls for another season and then for the San Diego Charms in the California Senior League for two seasons. Then I retired. I wanted to spend more time with Deljeet, and I was tired of all the travel.

It's not easy to just quit something that you have been doing your whole life. I had a couple of jobs in San Diego, but I sure missed hockey. I wanted to go back just one more time, so I did, in 1978-79. I played 53 games for the San Diego Hawks in the Pacific Hockey League. I'm pleased to say that I scored 21 goals and added 25 assists. Not too bad for a 43-year-old!

And then I quit hockey for good. Deljeet was pregnant, and I was going to be a father again. This time I vowed I was going to be home for the baby instead of chasing pucks all over the place. The question that kept me awake was: What do I do now?

CHAPTER NINETEEN

ONE MORE SHIFT

I had been a pro hockey player for 18 years. Suddenly, I wasn't one anymore. I had worked in the off-season, but now I needed a full-time job. Especially since our daughter Chandra was born in July 1979. So I got a job as an officer with Strategic Security, and we looked after security for the San Diego Chargers of the NFL. If I wasn't going to be a professional athlete, I was at least going to be around them.

Security for an NFL game is a big deal. I would leave the house early on game day, which was always Sunday (unless we were in the playoffs or on *Monday Night Football*). I would go to the stadium, and we would put our game plan together. I was the supervisor, and I would sit up in the command post with the fire marshal and police officers. We would watch the crowd on video screens and check in with each other on walkie-talkies, and we'd look at the crowd with binoculars. We also got to see the game. There were never any real problems — just rowdy drunks acting up sometimes. Even so, it was a long day. The game would start at 1 PM and would finish around 4. I would get home by 8 PM.

I was even licensed to carry a "concealed weapon," which means a gun that you wear under your suit jacket. I come from a country where hardly anybody owns a gun, so it was strange to be wearing a gun on the job. I'm happy to say I never had to use it.

I liked working security, and I moved on to the Hotel Del Coronado, on Coronado Island in San Diego. "The Del," as it's called, is one of the most spectacular hotels in the world. It's a huge white Spanish-style building right on the edge of the Pacific Ocean. It has white sandy beaches, tennis courts, swimming pools, huge outdoor patios, and wonderful gardens filled with all kinds of tropical plants and flowers.

Inside, it has beautiful wood paneling everywhere, and fine restaurants and bars, and first-rate shops. It's a very elegant place, and we would get lots of weddings and big fancy parties there, with lots of folks just passing through to take a look (although some of them were up to doing more than that, which is where I came in). I would walk between eight and 11 miles a day, keeping track of the action.

The Del has seen a lot of famous people visit since it was built in the 1880s. Thomas Edison, the great inventor, installed the electric lights himself. L. Frank Baum, who wrote *The Wizard of Oz*, stayed in the hotel while he wrote the book. Some people think that the turrets in Emerald City were inspired by those on top of the hotel. Many movies have been filmed there too. Someday you might see the most famous one, *Some Like It Hot*.

Even though I enjoyed my work, I still wanted to get back into hockey. I missed it something terrible. I thought a door had opened in 1990, when San Diego got a new hockey franchise. The city had been without hockey since 1978 — the same year that I retired for good. When I hung up my skates, the Hawks folded, too, and that was until 1990. Then, San Diego hockey fans had a cause to rejoice when the Gulls came to town with the International Hockey League. I rejoiced, too. Here was my opportunity to get back in the game. So I went down to see the Gulls and asked if there was chance of working for them. I was well-known in the community, and I figured I could help them out.

They said yes, so I worked in community relations, and ticket sales, and for seven years I was their top salesmen. I'd go to speak at schools to promote the Gulls. This turned out to be good training for what was coming next, although I didn't know it at the time.

In 1996, I was still working security at The Del and hoping to get back into hockey, but I was going on 61 years old. I figured my chances were slim at best. Then, just out of the blue, I received a phone call from Bryant McBride. Bryant is a young black man who was born in Chicago but raised in Sault Ste. Marie, Ontario, and he works in the NHL's head office in New York. In fact, he has two jobs. He's the Vice President of Business Development, but he also works for the NHL/USA Hockey Diversity Task Force. The Diversity Task Force is an organization that helps minority kids play hockey, and maybe even play pro hockey one day if they want to — if they're good enough.

Bryant had called me because he had a wonderful idea. He wanted to choose 24 hockey-playing kids from different ethnic communities — black or Latino or Asian — from all over North America and give them a treat. Bryant wanted to fly them to Boston to play in a special hockey tournament. He wanted to call it "The Willie O'Ree All-Star Weekend." And he wanted me to come, too.

I was surprised and flattered and excited. Imagine an All-Star Weekend for minority kids, and one named after me. It's something I never dreamed could happen. I told Bryant I'd have to get the time off at The Del. My boss knew that I was trying to get back into hockey, so when I asked him for time off, he said, "Go and have fun."

Boy, did I ever have fun! The kids were great. They played one game at a local rink, then one at the FleetCenter where the Bruins play. They showed all kinds of talent, and they were just in awe of playing on an NHL rink.

It was also great for me in another way because it was also the NHL All-Star Weekend, so I got to see many of the friends I had made 35 years earlier, when I played for the Boston Bruins. Fernie Flaman, Bronco Horvath, Fleming Mackell, Leo Boivin, and Johnny Bucyk were all there, and we had a great time remembering the old days and talking about the new ones. Bobby Orr was just great that weekend. He signed autographs all day long, until every kid, mother, grandmother, uncle, and cousin had his signature. He was such an inspiration to the kids and to myself — it was a pleasure being in his presence. The weekend went by far too fast, and I was sorry to leave.

Little did I know that I wasn't exactly leaving, I was just arriving. Bryant then asked me to go to Bellingham, Washington, to help Dr. Bob Osterman with a sports dinner he was hosting. Bob runs Creative Concepts, which uses hockey to help kids in trouble. Bob's kids have had problems with the law, and he uses hockey to teach them to control their anger. It's a great program, but he was worried that no one would show up to his dinner. So I went on the radio to help promote the banquet, and I even went to a juvenile detention center to speak to kids about his program. In the end, they had to put in more tables to fit all the people who showed up. It was a big success!

The following year, the NHL asked me to come to the next Willie O'Ree All-Star Weekend in Chicago. Again, I had to get time off, and my boss had to get someone to replace me. I was worried that I might lose my job. Then the next year, 1998, I was invited to the NHL All-Star Game in Vancouver. This time, though, the NHL had an even bigger surprise for me. Bryant said, "Willie, I've been talking to the NHL's commissioner, Gary Bettman. We have a question. What would it take for you to join the Diversity Task Force on a permanent basis?" I couldn't believe what I was hearing. The NHL and USA Hockey wanted to give me a job. I thought about it for a second and said, "Two weeks' notice."

What that meant was I needed to give two weeks' notice to my boss at The Del. Then I would be free and clear to join the NHL. After spending years as a player trying to get into the NHL, and then *back* into it, here I was getting another chance. At age 63. I had to laugh because I wouldn't have believed it if I had read it in a book. It was amazing. I was going to help minority kids find a dream and then live it. I was going to help them skate on the ice that I had skated on. I was going to be a pioneer once again.

CHAPTER TWENTY

FROM ME TO YOU

You might think that I have come a long way from Fredericton, New Brunswick, but in many ways, I have come back to where I started. Once, I was a minority kid who wanted to play hockey. Now, as director of the NHL/USA Hockey Diversity Task Force, I help other minority kids to play hockey.

It's easier now, in many ways, because the world is so much different. No one thinks twice if they see a black face on a hockey team. Guys like Mike Grier in Edmonton and Anson Carter in Boston are two of the NHL's rising young black stars. People don't boo them in the rinks — they cheer them! And that's the way it should be.

I still live in a suburb of San Diego called La Mesa, with my wife Deljeet and our daughter Chandra. And our malamute-cross dog, Maya, and our cat, Meena. I can't forget them. My job takes me away from my family for about 18 days each month — that's more than half a month — and almost all of February! It can seem like a very long time.

Sometimes the travel itself can be annoying. Waiting hours to change planes or being delayed because of bad weather can be frustrating. But once I'm working with the kids, none of that matters. I talk to kids five to 18 years old, and I get so excited to see faces from so many different ethnic backgrounds who all want to play hockey.

And they can play because hockey is booming everywhere. Twenty years ago in San Diego, there were 600 kids trying to get ice time in just one arena. It was so bad that they would have to start playing at 2:30 in the morning. The kids would be lucky if they could play twice a week. When I first started playing, I was on the ice every day. You have to skate that often if you ever want to be any good. But now there are rinks everywhere — Harlem in New York, Texas, Georgia, Carolina, Miami, Chicago, all over the place.

And they don't just have ice rinks. In-line rinks are big here in San Diego, and I was at the opening of in-line hockey rinks in New Orleans and Tampa not too long ago. It doesn't matter to me if kids are playing on ice or pavement. They just need to be able to play.

I love many things about my job, but what I love most is the excitement the kids have about playing the game. Like I did, they love feeling as if they're flying when they skate, the breeze whipping past them. They feel like they can do anything, and you know what — they can, and you can.

Kids who have never been out of their own inner-city neighborhoods are amazed that playing hockey gets them a ride on an airplane and a place at my All-Star Weekend. Kids who have never been given anything get free hockey equipment donated by the NHL and USA Hockey. Kids who have been in trouble at school or with the law find a place where they can be taught teamwork. As any hockey player knows, if you don't have teamwork, you don't have a team.

I waited 17 years to get back onto the hockey team, and I want to give back what hockey has given me. I have told you the things that happened to me — not to a friend, not to my brother — during my life. If you really feel that you want to accomplish something, you can do the impossible. Always be proud of who you are. You can't change the color of your skin so don't even think of it. When kids ask me what it was like when people called me names, I tell them, "I just looked at myself as a man, and people have to accept me as a hockey player because of my skills and ability."

There's a saying that I like a lot. "Each man is three men: what he thinks he is, what others think he is, and what he really is." Know who you really are and be true to yourself. Everything will flow smoothly after that. If I can just get that message through to one person, then I'm happy. That's even better than being the first black man to play in the NHL.